W9-BCO-144

LEARN TO RELAX

Dr. C. Eugene Walker holds a Ph.D. in Clinical Psychology. He is Associate Professor of Psychology at the University of Oklahoma Medical School and Director of the Outpatient Pediatric Psychology Clinic there. In addition, he maintains a private and consulting practice of psychology. He has contributed numerous articles to professional journals in the field of psychology.

LEARN TO
RELAX

13 ways to reduce tension

C. Eugene Walker

A SPECTRUM BOOK

Prentice-Hall, Inc., Englewood Cliffs, New Jersey

Library of Congress Cataloging in Publication Data

WALKER, CLARENCE EUGENE.
    Learn to relax.

    (A Spectrum Book)
    Includes index.
        1. Anxiety.   2. Relaxation.   3. Conduct of life.
    I. Title. [DNLM: 1. Anxiety—Therapy—Popular works.
    2. Relaxation—Popular works.   WM172 W177L]
    BF575.A6W34   131'.33   75-5859
    ISBN 0-13-527564-4
    ISBN 0-13-527556-3 pbk.

© 1975 by PRENTICE-HALL, INC.
Englewood Cliffs, New Jersey

A SPECTRUM BOOK

19   18   17   16   15   14   13   12   11

Printed in the United States of America

PRENTICE-HALL INTERNATIONAL, INC. *(London)*
PRENTICE-HALL OF AUSTRALIA PTY. LTD. *(Sydney)*
PRENTICE-HALL OF CANADA, LTD. *(Toronto)*
PRENTICE-HALL OF INDIA PRIVATE LIMITED *(New Delhi)*
PRENTICE-HALL OF JAPAN, INC. *(Tokyo)*
PRENTICE-HALL OF SOUTHEAST ASIA (PTE.) LTD. *(Singapore)*

CONTENTS

vii

PREFACE

A basic fact of life is that we all experience tension and anxiety as a part of our existence. Sometimes the experience is mild and passes quickly. Sometimes it is agonizingly severe and may last for long periods of time. This has always been so. Some think that the nature of our civilization and technology may be causing our tensions and anxieties to escalate at a rate faster than our ability to cope with them. It is impossible to know whether this is true or not. However, the basic fact of anxiety as a part of living remains with us. Psychologists have developed numerous ways to treat anxiety in those who come for help. In this book you will find these techniques, many of them quite recent, explained in such a way that you can use them yourself. These techniques have helped millions of people. It is my hope that they will be useful to you.

LEARN TO RELAX

WHAT IS ANXIETY?

Because anxiety is such a simple word and such a common experience to all people, it may come as a surprise that psychologists do not really know exactly what it is. In fact, some psychologists have argued that the term itself is so vague and so general that it is useless for precise communication. While this may seem like nonsense—psychology is sometimes called the science of making common sense unintelligible—there are problems in clearly defining what we mean by *anxiety*. The reason is that anxiety is a word that we use to cover a large number of situations. For example, a person may say to us that he is anxious. This may be a subjective feeling that he is reporting to us. We may or may not have guessed that he was feeling that way, depending on his outward behavior. If we ask further, we may find that his mind seems to be racing and is full of worries, fears, and ideas which keep recurring and tormenting him. He may have various physical sensations also, but they may not seem to be especially prominent. The anxiety seems to be centered in his head.

However, he might say that his mind or head is clear, but he is experiencing physical sensations or problems which he calls anxiety. These may include one or more of the following, as well as a host of others: muscular tightness, nausea, stiff neck, general or localized body pain, respiratory problems, rapid heartbeat, dry mouth, hot flashes, chills, sweating (especially on the hands), excessive urination, diarrhea, loss of appetite, and sleep disturbances.

On the other hand, he might deny any subjective feelings of anxiety and claim that none of the physical symptoms mentioned above are present. Yet we might insist that he is anxious if we note such things as changes in his normal speech patterns, skin flushing, distinctive facial expressions, tics or twitches, physical awkwardness, saying unusual things, stuttering, stammering, making mental errors, or having accidents. When I was a graduate student of psychology at Purdue University, we lived under a great deal of tension and anxiety about our studies and our futures. All graduate students feel such pressure. A standing joke with us was to walk up to a fellow student and ask him if he was anxious. The correct response to this question was to give a startled jump, purse the lips, and say "Nope."

Another situation that we would label anxiety is that of the student who "blocks" on exams. If a student is very tense about an exam, he may study diligently and know the material thoroughly before the test. However, when the test paper is in front of him, sometimes he finds to his consternation that his mind is blank; he cannot remember anything he studied. Generally, as soon as the exam hour is over, he finds that he can again remember it all. Some understanding instructors will let the student complete the exam, even though the time is up. Another way of handling this situation is for the student to quit trying for awhile. He should get a drink of water, take a short walk, sharpen a pencil, or do something of that sort. Often a person in such a situation is trying too hard. Breaking up his mental set lets him get a fresh start and get over the blocking.

If a person has one or any combination of the symptoms above, he might say he is anxious, or others might consider him to be anxious. In addition, at different times in his life or in response to different situations, he might show different patterns of these signs. We would label them all anxiety. To further complicate matters, studies of all these components indicate that different people experience different patterns and combinations of the above in the *same* situation. They would all say, however, that they were *anxious*.

So, the word does cover a multitude of experiences. Anxiety is everywhere and in everyone.

Since excessive anxiety is considered to be one of the major symptoms of neurosis, some clinicians have speculated that the nature of man may be to be neurotic, at least in civilized society as we know it today. Some ethologists and anthropologists argue that this is the case because in our evolutionary history, the survival of the "beast" known as man depended on a combination of physical aggressiveness and mental foresight. However, this "beast" now finds himself in a society that permits his powers of foresight to run wild (even feeds and exaggerates them with communicative media) but forbids the use of physical force or aggression as a solution to problems. Thus, man is a cornered animal and experiences a chronic state of anxiety (or neurosis) in our complex type of world. In the later chapters of this book, we will see that such a pessimistic prospect is not inevitable.

Since anxiety is such a vague term, it might be helpful to define several related terms that describe human experience in this area. Psychologists differ in their use of these terms depending on their ideas about personality and psychotherapy. The following definitions are simple ones that will do for our discussion.

While there is no completely adequate definition of **anxiety,** we might refer to it as the reaction we have to a situation where we believe our well-being is endangered or threatened in some way. This may be any form of well-being. We may feel that our physical safety is in danger, or our success in our job, or our self-esteem, or the well-being of someone important to us, as in the case of the parent anxiously waiting for a child to return from a date. To say a person is "nervous" is pretty much synonymous with saying he is "anxious." **Tension** may be thought of as chronic, usually low level, anxiety that is experienced as a part of an ongoing situation in which we are involved. **Fear** may be termed intense anxiety experienced in response to a specific threat.

A **phobia** is an intense incapacitating fear attached to a specific thing or situation. All people have some phobias, whether they are of blood, bugs, snakes, airplanes, or whatever. We used to give fancy Greek names to each phobia—claustrophobia (fear of enclosed places), acrophobia (fear of high places), hydrophobia (fear of water). However, clinicians now just label the problem as a phobia and state plainly what the object is. In chapter two we present a technique that eliminates phobias in a relatively short period of time.

Unconscious anxiety may mean many things, but basically, as we might expect, it is anxiety of which we are not consciously aware. For example, often we don't realize how tense or anxious we were about a matter until it has passed. The relief we feel at that moment makes us reflect on the past and decide that we were anxious at the time. However, we did not consciously label it such in our mind at the time it was occurring.

Free floating anxiety describes a situation where intense anxiety seems unexpectedly to attack a person, only to go away and return later. Generally, the person realizes that he is under a great deal of general tension or strain, but he is unable to connect specific events with the attacks.

Panic is a condition in which the anxiety has become so great that the person loses complete control of himself and the situation. The person often becomes confused and may do bizarre things. It is a very painful and unpleasant experience. Many emotionally disturbed people seem to live in a chronic state of panic or near panic. When we deal with them, it helps if we keep this in mind. Gentleness, patience, and help in structuring things so they can handle them can go a long way with such people.

From what we have said so far, we might get the idea that anxiety is the great enemy of modern man. This is only partly true, however. Anxiety is a lot like pain. We prefer to experience as little of it as possible, but it serves a very useful purpose in alerting us and activating our defenses in times of danger. Moderate amounts of anxiety motivate us to plan for future events and increase our ability to cope with situations as they occur. The increased strength of the person who is afraid or the person who admits he works better under a little pressure are examples of the beneficial nature of anxiety. I recall, when preparing for the major comprehensive examinations that would determine whether or not I would receive my degree in psychology, that I became much more mentally alert than usual. I found myself able to read faster than usual and developed almost a photographic memory for what I read which was not the usual case with me. Partly the occasion for this was created by the fact that the exams were given in January, and as one who considers athletics an art form, I could hardly spend much time preparing for the exams until the "repertory season" of football bowl games was completed.

It is when anxiety becomes excessive that it is a problem. Those who have studied human activation have noted that this is a common feature of many motivating forces. When they are moderate, increasing the amount leads to increased and better performance. However, eventually a peak is reached and any additional amount results in deterioration of the performance. This is certainly the case with anxiety. A little brings out the best in us. A life without emotions, anxiety included, would be very drab. However, too much is debilitating. This is part of the fascination of amusement parks. We can administer small amounts of anxiety to ourselves in controlled conditions and feel the joy of dissipating it immediately. Likewise thriller books and movies are fun because they excite and activate us with an exhilarating feeling in a situation which we know is really quite safe. The person who enjoys challenges does the same thing in real life. However, we would not enjoy amusement parks if our lives were really in great danger on every ride. Nor would we welcome challenges or tasks in our lives that we were not able to cope with. Such situations would be destructive and debilitating rather than pleasurable. Excessive anxiety inhibits and defeats us. We have all been frozen by fear or have been unable to perform simple functions in front of an audience that made us nervous.

I recall another amazing revelation of this effect of anxiety from my undergraduate days in college. I was taking a course in French and each day we were assigned translations to do at night and recite on the next day in class. I used to labor over these translations for hours each night, looking up each word, and puzzling over the syntax to make the translation as close to perfect as possible. It was always embarrassing to make a mistake in front of the whole class. One day I failed to get the translation done ahead of time and had decided to cut class. On the way across campus I ran into my French instructor. I explained to him that I had not had time to do the translation for the day and did not want to take his time without being prepared. He suggested that I come along anyway and just listen. However, when it was my turn to recite, he asked if I would like to try it even though I wasn't prepared. I decided I would, and found to my surprise that I was able to read the lesson without hesitation as though it were in English. I stopped only at words in the new vocabulary for the day and easily went on after they were supplied by the instructor. The fact is that by removing all pressure to perform and anxiety about being so precise, I was able to do better than ever. I felt no pressure, because after all, I hadn't prepared and couldn't be expected to do very well. I had never been able to do that before and have never been able to do it since. That was the only time I was able to approach a translation completely free of inhibiting anxieties.

In the chapters to follow we will present a number of specific ways to keep anxiety in check so that it enhances rather than inhibits performance. Anxiety is a fact of existence. It is best to learn to make it work for us rather than against us.

chapter two

SYSTEMATIC DESENSITIZATION

Many of the anxieties that people experience are due to what psychologists call **conditioned reactions.** Simply stated, what psychologists mean by this is that things that frequently occur together in our experience become linked or associated with each other so that we respond to them in the same, or a highly similar, way when they happen again. Thus, if we are made anxious or afraid in the presence of certain factors (psychologists refer to them as stimuli), these same factors or stimuli will make us anxious later when they occur, even if the situation in reality no longer poses an actual threat. For example, a person may have had a number of experiences as a child in which a person in authority, such as a school principal, policeman, or guard, frightened him and perhaps punished him in some way. His reaction as an adult to a person in authority may produce considerably more anxiety in him than the situation really calls for. This is because of his previous conditioning of strong anxiety to this type of person. A person, so conditioned, might be driving along a highway and see a police car pull up behind him. He may feel considerable anxiety at the approach of the car. If the policeman stops him, the driver may have many symptoms of anxiety such as a pounding heart, rapid respiration, muscular tenseness, stuttering, and stammering speech. Of course, this is an overreaction to the situation. He was breaking no law and the officer may only want to tell him that his tail light is broken or warn him of a road hazard ahead. At worst, he may have broken a minor traffic law which would cost a few dollars fine. However, for many, the situation evokes anxiety near panic. Such effects often result from conditioned reactions.

Many of our emotions seem to be largely based on such conditioned reactions. Conditioned reactions are somewhat similar to reflexes, but they are learned rather than inherited. Their automatic or "reflexive" character, however, explains why it is hard to discuss things rationally with someone who is emotionally involved in a situation. He is responding more with his conditioned reactions to the present stimuli than relating to the actual realities of the situation. It also explains why we can tell ourselves that the next time a situation occurs we are not going to let it upset us and are going to handle it a certain way, only to find that when it does occur, we respond pretty much as we always have. This is the nature of conditioned reactions.

Now, if many of our anxieties are conditioned reactions, what can we do about them? Are we the victims of our traumatic past, or can we overcome such anxieties? Fortunately, we can overcome them. In fact, they are amazingly easy to overcome if we work at them in the right way. For decades psychologists have studied conditioned reactions in research laboratories all over the world. A clinical procedure for eliminating such anxieties was developed by Dr. Joseph Wolpe, a psychiatrist, which makes use of the basic principles learned from research. It is called systematic desensitization. If done properly, it works almost every time.

Let's use the example of authority persons to see how to use systematic desensitization on your own. Suppose this is your problem. The first step would be to sit down with some index cards and on each card write a different situation or experience that causes you anxiety in this area. After you have a stack of cards, place them in order, with the one that causes least anxiety on top and the one that causes most anxiety on the bottom. Your list might look something like this (least anxiety causing at top, most at bottom):

1. Walking past and greeting one of the bosses at work who is only a little older than myself.

2. Walking past and greeting one of the bosses at work who is considerably older than myself—one with gray hair and a gruff but somewhat fatherly demeanor.

3. Encountering one of the bosses who is only a little older than myself in the coffee-break room, where we will have to talk and have coffee together.

4. Encountering one of the bosses who is considerably older than myself—with gray hair and a gruff but somewhat fatherly demeanor—in the coffee-break room, where we will have to talk and have coffee together.

5. Having one of the bosses who is only a little older than myself watch me, without seeming pleased or displeased, while I work.

6. Having one of the bosses who is considerably older than myself —with gray hair and a gruff but somewhat fatherly demeanor —watch me while I work—without seeming pleased or displeased.

7. Having one of the bosses who is only a little older than myself watch me while I work and seeming to be displeased with what I am doing.

8. Having one of the bosses who is considerably older than myself—with gray hair and a gruff but somewhat fatherly demeanor—watch me while I work and seem to be displeased with what I'm doing.

9. Having one of the bosses who is only a little older than myself watch me while I work and make a slightly critical comment to me after watching for a while.

10. Having one of the bosses who is considerably older than myself—with gray hair and a gruff but somewhat fatherly demeanor—watch me while I work and make a slightly critical comment to me after watching for a while.

11. Having one of the bosses who is only a little older than myself watch me while I work and make a very critical comment after watching for a while.

12. Having one of the bosses who is considerably older than myself—with gray hair and a gruff but somewhat fatherly

demeanor—watch me while I work and make a very critical comment after watching for a while.

13. Attending a conference in the office of one of the bosses who is only a little older than myself to discuss something about my work that should be improved.

14. Attending a conference in the office of one of the bosses who is considerably older than myself—with gray hair and a gruff but somewhat fatherly demeanor—to discuss something about my work that should be improved.

15. Attending a conference with several bosses both young and old to discusss something about my work that should be improved.

Next, you have to learn to relax completely. Believe it or not, you can actually train yourself to do this rather easily. First sit in a comfortable chair or lie on a couch or bed. Then say something like the following to yourself, "I am going to relax completely. First, I will relax my forehead and scalp. I will let all the muscles of my forehead and scalp relax and become completely at rest. All of the wrinkles will smooth out of my forehead and that part of my body will relax completely. Now, I will relax the muscles of my face. I will just let them relax and go limp. There will be no tension in my jaw. Next, I will relax my neck muscles. Just let them become tranquil and allow all of the pressure to leave them. My neck muscles are relaxing completely. Now, I will relax the muscles of my shoulders. That relaxation will spread down my arms to the elbows, down the forearm to my wrists, hands, and fingers. My arms will just dangle from the frame of my body. I will now relax the muscles of my chest. I will let them relax. I will take a deep breath and relax, letting all of the tightness and tenseness leave. My breathing will now be normal and relaxed, and I will relax the muscles of my stomach. Now I will relax all of the muscles up and down both sides of the spine; now the waist, buttocks, and thighs down to my knees. Now the relaxation will spread to the calves of my legs, my ankles, feet, and toes. I will just lie here and continue to let all of my muscles go completely limp. I will become completely relaxed from the top of my head to the tip of my toes."

If you try this one or two times, you will be amazed at just how relaxed you can become. If you have trouble doing this at first, you might try purposely tensing the muscles of various parts of your body a few times and then letting them relax completely immediately following the forced tension. This will teach you to discriminate clearly between the tense and relaxed state, and train you in producing relaxation at will. Go through each of the muscle groups mentioned above (forehead and scalp, face, neck, shoulders, etc.) and learn to relax them one by one. You may spend three or four sessions just working on this. Then go through the whole procedure in one sitting. You will find yourself very relaxed at this point.

After you are completely relaxed, you are ready to begin the systematic desensitization. Take the top card from the pile and look at it. Then close your eyes and visualize the situation described on it as vividly as you can in your imagination. Imagine it occurring and imagine that you are really there. As you do that, you may experience some anxiety. If so, *stop* the imaginary scene *at once* and go back to relaxing. Relax all of the muscles again. Generally, taking just a deep breath or two and letting all of the muscles rest will do the job. However, if you need to, go through the whole relaxation sequence in your mind again, muscle by muscle.

When you are again completely relaxed, wait a few seconds. Then look at the card and imagine the scene once more. If you feel anxiety, make your mind turn blank, stop imagining the scene and go back to relaxing. Do this over and over until you can imagine the scene without feeling anxiety. It may take only a couple of times, or it may take 15—20 times, but repeat it until you can imagine the scene without feeling anxiety. When you have accomplished this, go on to the second scene. Continue in this manner until you have gone through all the cards.

It is best to work on the scenes like this for about a half an hour at a time. You may want to do it every day or every other day or only a couple of times a week, depending on your schedule and how quickly you want to conquer the anxiety. Usually, from one session to the next, it is a good idea to start by going over the last item or two from the previous session that you were able to imagine without anxiety.

A variation of the above procedure, which some people use, is tape recording a vivid description of the scene in advance. They then relax and listen to the tape. If they feel anxious, they shut the tape off and relax. When calm, they back the tape up and begin again.

When you have completed the above process, you will find that situations which used to cause stabbing pains of anxiety at their mere thought can now be calmly thought about without disturbance. You have been desensitized. To make the treatment complete, you should now calmly go over in your mind what is the right thing to do in the situation that has caused you anxiety. Then make plans to actually do the right thing the next time the situation occurs. You will be amazed to find that your previous anxiety kept you so uptight that you avoided thinking or planning in this area; it prevented you from thinking clearly when you were in the situation. This will all be different now. It is a good idea, as you desensitize yourself to the scenes on the cards, to plan how to handle such situations and then seek out several occasions when you can practice doing better. Some people go through the relaxation procedure just before confronting the real situation. Others just take a deep breath and get as relaxed and composed as they can. Many of my patients have been so elated by the effects of this treatment that they have deliberately sought situations which previously caused them great anxiety, frustration, and failure.

Once you have desensitized yourself to the situations and experienced them a few times in real life, you will find that they are actually conquered and cause you no discomfort at all. It may seem almost too good to be true, but it does work.

If you have trouble going through the procedure alone, you might want to enlist the help of a friend. Often you can arrange to help each other by trading roles and desensitizing one another. If you do this, have the friend instruct you step by step to relax all of the muscles and then vividly describe the scene to you while you stay relaxed. You will need to tell the friend enough details about the scene so that he can weave an imaginary story, one you can really put yourself into and experience. If you feel anxiety, at any time, signal the friend by raising the index finger of your right hand. He should, at that instant, tell you to turn off your imagination, make your mind go blank, and return to relaxing. When you are relaxed, he can begin again.

Another way of handling conditioned anxiety that works just as well as the preceding method in most cases, and better in some, is called *in vivo* desensitization. The term *in vivo* simply means in this case, "in real life." To do this you again make a list of situations and arrange them in order as before. This time, however, skip the imagination part and simply plan in advance how to handle each situation. Then seek out the least anxiety-provoking situation, relax and carry out your plan. Analyze the results after each try and figure out better ways to respond and handle the situation the next time. Then do it again. Repeat this until you conquer one item on the list, then go on to the next and the next until you are comfortable with each and can handle all of them. Remember that "He who would move mountains must start with the pebbles at the foot of the hill."

As an example of real life desensitization, suppose you have a lot of anxiety in social situations. After thinking about it you might develop a hierarchy that looks like this (least anxiety-causing at top, most at bottom):

1. Making small talk with a stranger, for example, at a bus stop.

2. Having a fairly extended conversation with a stranger, for example, in the doctor's waiting room.

3. Meeting a new person for the first time and talking only briefly with him, for example, being introduced to him by a mutual friend on the street as you happen to run into each other.

4. Meeting a new person at a party and having to make conversation with him for a few minutes.

5. Meeting several new people at a party and making small talk.

6. Meeting a new person who joins you and some mutual friends for dinner.

7. Meeting several new people who join you and some mutual friends for dinner.

8. Being the only new person who must meet several people for the first time and have dinner with them, for example, being placed at a table of strangers at a dinner party.

The way to attack the above problem would be to take the first item and look for naturally occurring occasions or even arrange for occasions to occur in which you can experience the event. You should prepare for the occasion in a way that is logical and appropriate. Being prepared is half the battle. In the above example, you might make it a point to read the newspaper in order to glean some topics to talk about. You might go over in your mind various pleasantries that seem to contribute to a congenial encounter. You might have an appropriate joke or anecdote in the back of your mind. You might search the other person's interests, once you meet, for one you share. A compliment on how he looks or on something he said will seldom lead you astray and will often make him a friend for life. The point is, plan in advance how you will handle the occasion. Then when you are in the situation, work out what you have planned. As a boy, I used to work on a truck farm. The foreman had a large sign on the blackboard at the barn which read, "Plan the work and work the plan." It's good advice.

Just before you enter the situation, go through the relaxation procedure or, at least, take a few deep breaths, shrug your shoulders, and get completely relaxed. Then go in and do the best you can.

After it is over, think about and analyze how things went. Learn from each experience how to perform better next time. Then do it again. Eventually, the anxiety will be gone and you will have developed a repertoire of skills in handling such situations. At that point, you will no longer need the elaborate plans. It will just come "naturally."

Be sure to start with the least anxiety-provoking situation. Go on to the next highest and the next only after the ones below it have been conquered. Success depends on a careful, systematic attack.

Looking at the example above, you can see that it deals with social situations involving strangers. Obviously you could make up similar hierarchies involving friends or involving different types of socialization (e.g., parties, job interviews, public speaking) or a variety of other things. Most people have been conditioned to react with anxiety to enough things so that they may make up several hierarchies dealing with different things and work through them. If you have more than one hierarchy at a time which you want to work on, you can work a little on each in every session or go through one completely in a series of sessions and then begin the next.

Some people have used an approach that is in between the imagination approach and the real-life approach discussed above. It is called behavioral rehearsal. In this, you rehearse things with a friend that you would like to do without anxiety. For example, in a job interview, have a friend play the part of the interviewer. He can play the part of different kinds of interviewers (stern, hostile, friendly, etc.), and you can practice being calm and responding to the questions. At the end, you can discuss how you might have better handled the situation. Then, try it again. Do it over and over until you act without anxiety. The different types of interviews and different types of interviewers can be arranged in hierarchies and worked on using this method.

The hardest part of using these procedures is developing the hierarchies. Often just what it is that makes us anxious seems vague, hard to define or to separate out from other factors. The basic strategy is to keep the scenes as simple and straightforward as possible. The best way to start is simply to write down on cards as many situations that involve anxiety as possible without worrying about categories or hierarchies. After you have done that, sort them out into logical categories involving one dimension or a couple of dimensions that seem to go together well. Each of these piles will become a hierarchy of its own. Read over all the items in a given pile and fill in the gaps by writing new cards that obviously would fit in with the ones already written. Extend the range upward and downward by making up more or less extreme situations. Eventually, you will develop a hierarchy with 10 to 25 items. If you have too many more than that, break it into two or more hierarchies.

Many times people also wonder if they are including the "right" things in their hierarchies. The best way to handle this is to make them as specific and as close to real life as you can. If they are specific, real-life situations that make you anxious, they are right for the hierarchy.

When you start the desensitization procedure, if you have trouble staying relaxed and getting past the first item on the hierarchy, you have started out with one that is too threatening. Write some less anxiety-provoking items and extend your list downward. If you reach a point at which you have conquered the last item but the next one on the list seems not to be getting any better, say after 15 or 20 trials, you probably have made too big a jump. Write some additional items that would logically fit in between the two and work on them.

Sometimes we have anxiety about an event that doesn't seem to have a logical hierarchy to go with it. Often this is a very unique event, sometimes one that will happen only once in our lives. For example, your upcoming wedding might be causing anxiety. The way to use the systematic desensitization procedure for such events is to imagine the whole event, step by step, from beginning to end while staying relaxed. At the first sign of anxiety, stop, make your mind turn blank, then go back to the beginning and start over. Keep this up until you can imagine the whole thing without anxiety. You will find yourself much more relaxed when the event actually occurs than if you had not done this.

One further tip. Imagination, behavioral rehearsal, and *in vivo* desensitization all work on essentially the same principle. We generally use the imagination and rehearsal procedures for situations that don't occur often enough in real life to make the *in vivo* system practical or when the situation is so anxiety provoking that we are too terrified to try it in real life.

The procedures presented in this chapter work well and can be applied to a large number of anxieties in various areas of life. Since they are based on research findings, they must be done correctly to work. Some people have trouble knowing how to get started or run into difficulties along the way. If this happens, it is best to consult a professional psychologist for assistance. Often he will be able to give you some advice on how to handle the problems you are having so that you can continue on your own. Sometimes he may feel that your situation is sufficiently difficult that it would be best for you to see him regularly for a period of time to work on the problems under his care and direction. To find such a psychologist, call the chairman of the psychology department at a nearby university and ask him for the names of psychologists or psychiatrists in your area who practice behavior therapy using systematic desensitization.

chapter three

RELAXATION EXERCISES

Everyone who has gazed at the product of a "Mr. America"-type body-building program or who has watched a skilled athlete perform has been impressed with what can be done to develop and train the muscles of the body through regular, diligent practice. Recent developments in the field of psychology indicate that considerable conscious control can also be exerted over basic physiological processes which were previously thought to be more or less automatic and not subject to such intentional control. Patients have been taught to control heart rate, blood pressure, body temperature, brain waves, and other functions through training. The technique is generally referred to as biofeedback. The basic strategy is to arrange for the individual to receive some type of recognizable feedback when the body process is going in the desired direction and a different type of feedback when it isn't. For example, if a person was trying to slow his heart rate, he might be hooked up to an apparatus that would monitor heart rate and indicate by a blip of light on a TV-like screen what the heart rate was doing. The screen typically has a stripe down the middle. The blip is set to appear on that stripe to start with. If the heart rate slows down, the blip moves to the left. If it begins to increase, the blip moves to the right. By giving the person this kind of feedback, it is rather easy to train him to slow his heart rate down considerably. In certain types of illness, of course, that is very important. Use of biofeedback techniques requires expensive equipment and highly trained personnel to operate it.

However it is possible to train yourself rather simply to relax your muscles. This does not require expensive equipment or trained personnel. You can learn it easily on your own. If relaxation procedures are practiced with regularity, the level of tension and anxiety can be reduced significantly. These procedures may be thought of as relaxation *exercises*. Just as physical exercise trains and strengthens the muscles, making it possible for us to accomplish physical activities that we could not do otherwise, relaxation exercises increase our ability to tolerate stress and to remain calm in the face of life's pressures and problems. This is a crude analogy, of course, but it is helpful to think about it in these terms. The nervous system does not increase in size or change in the way the muscles do with exercise. However, with a program of relaxation exercises, the nervous system's functional capacity does change in a way that is very similar.

Many anxious people feel fairly well in the morning but find themselves becoming more and more tense as the day wears on. By the end of the day they are so tied in knots that they can't enjoy their evening meal. They later find themselves sitting in agony in front of the TV with heartburn, muscular tightness in the chest and back, nausea, a splitting headache, and a general feeling of pain and discomfort. They are unable to relax. What causes this is that, during the day, minor threats and problems generate tension and anxiety. This makes them uncomfortable and makes them worry about the fact that they are not feeling well and whether there will be more threats and problems as the day wears on and . . . tomorrow. They begin to wonder if they will be able to cope with them indefinitely. Thus, problems, tension, and worry develop into a closed loop system that maintains itself rather than being dissipated. The net result is a spiral effect, with anxiety increasing at a steady pace, until it is almost unbearable by the end of the day. To stop this process it is necessary to interrupt the feedback, thus breaking the spiral.

One of the simplest ways to accomplish this is to use the

relaxation procedure discussed in chapter two. Do this as an exercise, just the way you would do a physical exercise if you wanted to get in top physical shape. You should do it three or four times a day, every day. Once at midmorning, once at noon, once in the evening, and once at bedtime are the best occasions. Go through the procedure of relaxing all the muscles and then stay relaxed for three to five minutes. After that, you can get up and go about your business. You will find that you are much more relaxed and calm following the exercise. The exercise should only take you five minutes each time or a total of 15 to 20 minutes per day. The payoff in reduced anxiety leading to a happier and longer life is well worth the effort.

Some people find it difficult to find time to do the exercise. If you work at a job where you get coffee breaks, that is a good time. You will still have time for your coffee afterwards. If you don't have coffee breaks, you can go to the restroom at an appropriate time, find a comfortable seat and go through the procedure there. All jobs have provision for going to the restroom. Also, if you work in a busy place, the restroom is the best place to do the exercise. Usually it is quieter there and more privacy is afforded.

Again, the exercise interrupts the feedback loop that is causing the anxiety to spiral. The spiral effect ceases, allowing the anxiety to dissipate. Instead of steadily increasing anxiety until you are in misery by the end of the day, you return periodically to a calm resting state and start over. At the end of the day you are much more relaxed and less fatigued.

The above exercise can also be used before some type of recreational activity. For example, you can sit down and go through the exercise just before reading a book or watching a TV program. You will then find yourself very relaxed and more able to enjoy the recreation.

Another useful variation is to perform the exercise and then allow yourself to drift off into a nap. You will awaken very relaxed and refreshed. This also is an excellent technique to combat insomnia. To use it for insomnia, get in bed and go through the procedure as indicated. After you are fully relaxed, slowly think the word *sleep* over and over in your mind. Generally, I teach this to a patient in my office. The next time he returns for his appointment, I ask him how it went. The answer is usually "It worked very well. In fact, after the first time or two I never got to the end. I fell asleep in the middle."

Once you have learned to relax using the procedure above, you will often be able to get into the completely relaxed state in a matter of seconds, without going through each set of muscles from head to toe. You will need only to sit or lie in a comfortable position, take a deep breath, exhale, and let all your muscles go limp. The relaxation will be almost instantaneous. This is obviously an ability well worth cultivating. However, it does take diligent, systematic effort, just as does developing a muscular physique.

Some people like to make these relaxation exercises more interesting by using techniques of meditation along with the relaxation. There are numerous approaches to meditation, most of which derive from oriental philosophy and religion. Scientific research with these techniques has indicated that they do in fact affect bodily and mental processes in beneficial ways when practiced correctly. People who practice them are often able to achieve a considerable degree of bodily relaxation and mental calmness. They also report that they are emotionally very rewarding experiences leading to deeper insight into themselves and their surroundings.

If you want to try these techniques, you must first get in the right position. The lotus position is the most common one. Sit on the floor and cross your legs so that your right foot rests on your left thigh and your left foot rests on the right thigh. Next, make your back into a straight column, resting on the base of your legs and buttocks, so that it is comfortable and requires no strain to keep the back straight. If you put a pillow under your buttocks, this usually will give you a firm, comfortable base. Keep your head and neck comfortably erect. Rest your hands in your lap. The eyes may be kept open and focused at a point a few feet in front of the body, or they may be closed.

This position is, of course, rather difficult for many people to assume. If you have that problem, get as close to it as you comfortably can and then *gently* stretch the muscles each time you do the exercise. Eventually you will be able to do it.

An alternative is generally referred to as the "tailor" position. For this one, sit with your buttocks on a cushion and fold the legs in front of you so that the right foot is under the left knee and the left foot under the right knee. Still another possibility is to sit in a straight-backed chair, with your feet firmly on the floor, back and head erect, arms in the lap. Choose the one that best fits your anatomy and physical condition. It is important that you be comfortable.

Once in position, sway back and forth awhile to get completely comfortable. Then, take a few deep breaths. With each breath, let go a little and allow your muscles to relax. Mentally you should begin to clear your mind of the business and rushing that characterizes our lives. Begin to adopt a passive, detached attitude of observation. Do not try to achieve a certain state or to guide your thinking. Just let the attitude grow.

Having done this, you are ready for specific meditation exercises. One Taoist exercise directs the person to concentrate attention on the center of the torso at about the level of the navel. Thoughts, as they arise, should be "placed" at this level of the body and consciousness should be shifted to the solar plexus. Thoughts take on a different meaning and one develops a different awareness when things are experienced in this manner. This particular exercise has been the occasion for considerable ridicule about people who sit and contemplate their navels, but if practiced correctly it is a stimulating experience for many.

Another exercise is to concentrate on the feelings and sensations of the body and on the fact of existence as a being. Or, you can observe the process of your mind at work in thought. Watch your thoughts develop, feel them, and see how they are formed. Sometimes you may want to take an object and see it as an existence equivalent to yourself. You may want to meditate on a particular person, physically present with you or not. You may sometimes want to take a significant object from your past with pleasant connotations and meditate on it—such things as an old photograph, a school paper, a flower from your scrapbook, or some similar object.

Some people find it very pleasant to take a fantasy trip while meditating. If you want to do this, think about a place you have been that you liked a great deal. Re-experience it. Transport yourself mentally to the spot. See what is going on. You can concentrate on seeing it exactly as it was when you were there or on how you think it would be now. You can concentrate on the scenery such as forests, mountains, lakes, or on the people. Visualize the people in the place one by one and meditate on them.

You can meditate, in similar fashion, about a place you would someday like to visit. You can mentally transport yourself to the place and experience it, perhaps, in an even deeper way than going there. Later, going to the place is much more rewarding than it otherwise would have been. If you have a photograph or painting, these can be used as part of the above exercise.

An interesting exercise is to establish a pattern of slow, deep breathing. After you have established this pattern, think of the number one as you exhale. Then, take a breath and think of the number two. Do this until you have reached 10 or 15. A variation of this that you can try in a later exercise is to mentally place the numbers beside and on top of each other in your stomach as you exhale. Keep them there and note how you feel that the mind has shifted to the center of your body. This is a classic Zen technique.

You may find meditating to a certain sound interesting. One way to do this is to listen to some music you like. Experience it, feel it, go with it wherever it takes you. You may want to let your body move with the music. This is often an exhilarating experience.

Many people like to chant during their meditation. A mantra is a sacred sound which, in some forms of Buddhism, is passed from the master to his disciple. In India the greatest mantra is "Om." It is said to represent God in all His fullness. To use this chant, think of Om as divided into three separate syllables of equal length. Take a deep breath, as you exhale, make the sound "owww" as in *cow,* then slide into "ooou" as in *blue,* and then into "mmmm." Take another breath and do it again. Do this for a few minutes. Some people liken the effect to an internal massage. They also report calmness and expanded consciousness following. You may, of course, use other standard chants or develop your own.

Many people like to pray during their meditative exercises. Prayers should be focused on one simple idea or short passage from a religious writing. Think about what this means and how it can apply to your life. In meditation one can develop a deep inner communication with and sense of the presence of God.

Many other people find meditating on a poem or a line from a poem rewarding. A passage from a book can serve the same purpose. Many oriental and Western writers who meditate have written of their reflections and experiences. These can be very useful as material for meditation and reflection.

You may want to meditate on a koan (kō′-on). A koan is a seemingly nonsensical question which serves as a stimulus and focus for meditation. The word *koan* literally means a public document or a statement. It refers to a declaration that a master makes to his disciple for the disciple's instruction. There are many right answers to a koan and yet there is no answer. The koan makes us aware of the limits of words and the depths of mind and existence. For example, one that has had considerable popularity in this country is, "You have heard the sound of two hands when they clap together. What is the sound of one hand? What is this sound for 1,000?"

Other such koans are: "Show me your face before your father and mother were born" or "Where do we meet after you are dead, cremated, and the ashes are all scattered around?" Another is, "All things are said to return to One. Where, then, is the ultimate home of this One?" Sometimes the koan takes the form of a command which is paradoxical as in, "Use your spade which is in your empty hands," or "Walk while riding a donkey." Many times they take the form of seemingly nonsensical answers to questions: "Who is Buddha?" Answer, "Three pounds of flax"; or "What is the essence of Buddhism?" Answer, "My what a large melon this is." One famous koan was for the master to hold up his walking stick in front of his disciples and say, "This is not a stick. What do you call it?"

Most of the exercises discussed above can be done in a half hour to an hour on a daily basis. It is not necessary to do them every day, but a disciplined, regular use of them brings the best results. Beginners should not make the sessions too long.

For those interested in meditation, more information may be found in the public library or bookstores. The interested person may want to look into Zen, Yoga, transcendental meditation, Ta'i Chi, and similar areas. One of the better basic books for beginners is, *The Three Pillars of Zen* by Philip Kapleau, but there are many other excellent books available.

A word of caution is in order. Many people find meditation exercises beneficial, if properly practiced. However, they can also be upsetting to some people. If you feel that they would be upsetting, don't do them. For those who do these exercises, it is best to start out gradually and go only as far as you can with comfort. It is also best to work with and be supervised by someone with training and experience in the area.

One final relaxation exercise to be discussed is sometimes referred to as differential relaxation. It is very easy to understand and, with a little practice, can be readily employed. The basic point is that if we are sitting, standing, walking, running, or whatever, there are muscle groups that could be relaxed, while the others work. We tend to tense and work many muscles throughout the day that could be in a state of relaxation. We do this because we typically involve our whole selves in what we are doing. Sometimes, though, we may be overdoing it. It is obvious that while sitting, many muscles could be relaxed. But, even while running or walking, the arms, shoulders, back, and facial muscles, for example, could be relaxed. Analyze your daily activities and see how much relaxation can be worked in. Then discipline yourself to keep muscles relaxed rather than tensed when possible. Disciplining yourself is the difficult part. You will keep forgetting. However, if you learn to practice differential relaxation, you will see a general reduction of your tension and anxiety level, leaving you with a lot more energy and vitality at the end of a day. A physician, Edmund Jacobson, has written extensively on the use of this and other relaxation procedures for the reduction of anxiety. He finds them very successful with patients who are tense. A couple of his more helpful books are *Anxiety and Tension Control: A Physiologic Approach* and *You*

Must Relax: A Practical Method of Reducing the Strains of Modern Living.
Remember, if you want to develop physical strength, physical exercise is the way to do it. If you want to relax and reduce anxiety, the exercises outlined in this chapter can contribute a great deal toward that goal.

chapter four

STRAIGHT THINKING

Many anxieties arise from thoughts we have or interpretations of events in our lives that we know, intellectually, should not be anything to worry about. We tell ourselves that a certain situation is not so crucial; that there are many ways to look at it; and that it shouldn't bother us. And yet it does bother us. It can haunt and nag us daily, causing anxiety, irritability, and misery. Friends reassure us and we tell them we know that what they are saying is true, but we still can't get it out of our head. Sometimes, in cases like this, the main problem is faulty thinking. If we can think clearly and straighten things out in our mind, the problem dissolves.

A psychologist, Dr. Albert Ellis, has studied this aspect of anxiety for many years. He has developed a system of counseling and psychotherapy based on the idea of straight thinking. He calls his treatment rational-emotive therapy.

Often to make the technique of his therapy clear, he refers to the ABC's of emotional problems in the following manner. Generally when an Activating Event (A) occurs, it seems to cause an emotional reaction or Consequence (C) in a person. But, on closer examination, we may find that A did not, in fact, cause C. What caused C was the Belief System (B) of the person. Thus, we have the ABC's of anxiety. We will get to D when we talk about the remedy for this situation.

First, let's look at a couple of examples of how this can happen in everyday life. Suppose a person does a bad job at work. That is A. That is the fact of what happened. Often this activates a Belief System that runs something like this, "I did a bad job today. Isn't that horrible. I *always* do that. I'm really incompetent at everything I do. I'll never succeed. I'm a wretch. Most people know that about me. Probably, nobody really respects me. I'll never be accepted or have any friends to speak of." The emotional Consequence of this, of course, is anxiety, depression, and loss of self-esteem. But, as Dr. Ellis would point out to such a person, this is *catastrophizing*. We are overreacting to the facts of the situation, and because of our faulty Belief System, we actually produce a catastrophic Consequence. This is irrational. If we could be rational about it, we wouldn't feel that bad at all.

Let's look at another example. Suppose a normal, average, likable teen-age boy asks a girl for a date and she turns him down. This might activate a Belief System that says the following, "She doesn't like me well enough to go out with me even once. I must not be much of a man. All girls probably feel that way about me. This is awful. I'm a lousy excuse for a person. I'll never find the right girl to marry." Of course, the result, again, is anxiety, depression, and rumination about, "Who am I?" This is a common reaction among young adults and sometimes older ones too.

If that were all that happened, it would be bad enough. But it usually gets worse. The person left anxious and depressed by this small event in his life often finds that his reaction to the event is an Activating Event for other false Belief Systems which cause additional emotional Consequences. He continues in this way to dig a deeper and deeper hole for himself which he'll never get out of if something doesn't happen to stop it. Eventually, this kind of process results in the person being preoccupied with himself and distracted from meeting his responsibilities in life. He becomes tired and inefficient.

However, there is a solution. A person doesn't have to be victimized by these irrational Belief Systems. The answer is in learning to successfully Dispute (D) them. This calls for clear, rational thinking. Let's go back to the man who did a bad job at work that day. He could say something like this to himself, "I did a bad job today. Well, you win some and you lose some. Everybody has some good days and some bad days. The important thing in life is to *learn* from failure. Everybody fails and does a bad job sometimes. Nobody is exempt from that. The really successful people are the ones who learn from their mistakes and go back and do a better job the next time. Let me see. What can I learn from today? How can I do better tomorrow?" After some thought, he might say, "I feel better now. I think I'm going to get better at my job all the time."

Our boy who was turned down for the date might say to himself, "She doesn't want to date me now. Maybe she will some other time. There could be a lot of reasons for her saying no. Even if she doesn't like me at all, there are many other girls I can date. All boys are turned down by someone in their lives. It's really a minor thing. Someday I'll meet the right girl, and we'll get along fine."

Of course, the points made in this chapter involve mental processes. They are intended to combat *irrational* Belief Systems that cause us anxiety, and a great deal of our anxiety is caused by just such beliefs. However, behavior is part of it too. Along with the clear thinking, we need to be *doing* the right things and improving our actual performance all the time.

Many people find information to Dispute irrational Belief Systems by reading autobiographies of well-known people. It often helps eliminate irrational beliefs if we learn that others, even very famous people, have had the same thoughts or feelings from time to time that we have had. It also helps to discover that the same kinds of problems and events occur in such people's lives. For example, Louis Pasteur failed the admission exams for the University of Paris and did not get admitted on his first try. Even after he got in, he was regarded as a rather mediocre student and somewhat of a plodder by his professors. Albert Einstein once failed an elementary math course. Thomas Edison was expelled from school as uneducable. Dwight Eisenhower was a constant discipline problem at West Point and was almost expelled on more than one occasion. Johnny Unitas was cut from the Baltimore Colts the first time he tried out. One could go on, with an endless list of authors who got hundreds of rejection slips before ever getting anything in print, artists who weren't recognized until after they died, etc. The important thing to remember is that all people have setbacks. These events don't have to have catastrophic consequences if we think rationally about what has indeed occurred and what it means. These events can be a stimulus for growth and improvement if we see them as such, rather than provoking anxiety that leads to deterioration.

In analyzing Western culture, Dr. Ellis has identified twelve ideas that are very prevalent, but that are stupid, irrational, and lead to problems in our thinking.

1. We must be loved by everyone and everyone must approve of everything we do. This leads to much irrational concern on our part, especially when there are signs that somebody, anybody, doesn't like us or disapproves of something we are doing. This is a stupid position to take because it is not possible for everyone to like us. Nobody can please everybody. The very things that make one liked and approved of by one person, make him despised by another. To try to be loved by everyone only makes a person less self-directing, more insecure, and less interesting. It is desirable to be loved, and it is necessary to be sensitive to feedback from others in order to relate to them better; but one should not try to be loved by everyone. Rather, he should actively seek out other people who share sufficient interests and values with him so that he will get along well with them. It is better to spend our energy selecting and cultivating real friends than in trying to please everybody and anybody.

In counseling young people, I frequently find that while they are in the public school system, they often feel that they want to be popular with everyone at school. This creates a very great problem. The range of interests, socioeconomic levels, family backgrounds, etc., are so great that this is impossible. Yet, they are thrown in with this large group every day, and they want to be approved of by them. The problem frequently diminishes after they get out of school because they can selectively associate with people of tastes and values similar to their own.

In general it is best to maintain our own personal integrity, being true to our own values, while striving to be loving, creative, productive, and contributing individuals. If we do that, we can let people like us or not as they choose and not be overly anxious about it. We will have more real friends and be less plagued by irrational anxiety if we do so.

2. We must be thoroughly competent, adequate, intelligent, and achieving in all possible respects. It is obviously not possible to be perfect at everything. It is even impossible to really be *perfect* at anything. A person who sets such standards for himself is constantly full of anxiety about his past failure to achieve such perfection or that he will fail to achieve such perfection in the future. Even when he is acknowledged by others as being the best in an area (note that this is not the same as being *perfect*), he is constantly anxious because tomorrow he may fall from this position. He may decline or a new and better challenger may appear. People with this irrational belief often achieve a lot, but they generally don't enjoy it. Often the methods they use to achieve their success alienate others from them. In the long run, many such people do not really achieve their full potential because of their faulty Belief System. It is best to realize that we are not, and will not be, deities. We can't be more than human. Nobody, including ourselves, should expect that of us. We should strive for achievement and accomplishment. But, we should do this in the sense of making progress, learning, and growing as we go. Recognizing all the time that as humans we will make mistakes; we will fail; we will have faults; and we will be subject to limitations and fallibilities. We won't be perfect, but we will do what we can and will learn as we go along. That is all anybody has a right to ask of us.

3. Certain acts are wrong or wicked or villainous, and people who perform them should be severely punished. There are no absolute rights or wrongs. There are things that people do that we wouldn't do; things they do that we consider inappropriate or antisocial; and things we wish they wouldn't do. However these people are not bad people. Simply blaming them does no good. Punishing them does little, if any, good and often does harm. If we analyze why they did something, we can almost always see the sense of it from their point of view. Thus, their actions could be expected. If they were "wrong" (at least as we view things) in what they did, it is generally due to stupidity, ignorance, or emotional disturbance; so we should be very tolerant of their behavior and try to educate, redirect, and help them change to more desirable behavior. If we do so, we all come out ahead in the end.

Likewise, we should give ourselves the same break. If someone doesn't like what we do, we should not become anxious or upset about it. We should recognize that, within their framework, our behavior seems inappropriate. We should not be blamed for that. Nor should we become anxious and depressed about it. The rational thing to do is to compare ideas, discuss it, and see if we can learn from the experience. One or both of us may change, or we may agree to disagree, but we do better that way than by engaging in blaming and mutual hostility over a period of time that leaves us both losers.

4. It is a terrible catastrophe when things are not as we would like them to be. It is silly and childish when we think about it clearly, but many times we do proceed with the implicit assumption that the world and everything in it should be just the way *we* want it to be. We are deeply offended and outraged by all signs that it is not so. However, with all the different kinds of people in the world, it could not possibly be to everyone's liking. Also, the harsh reality of the universe is that it was not created only for our pleasure and to revolve around us personally. Therefore, we have to accept that the world, even our corner of it, will never be exactly the way we would like it. We should not expect it to be. When we see something we don't like, it does no good to perceive it as a personal insult or an attempt to defeat us. What one should do is to say, "That is too bad" or "I don't like that," and then try to do something constructive to change or improve it. As someone has said, if you are unavoidably dealt a lemon in life, you may as well make some lemonade. On the other hand, if it can't be improved at all, then we should resign ourselves to accepting it, realizing that this is sometimes the nature of things. We often tell our children that they have to realize that they can't have everything they want.

Sometimes, though, as adults we make the same error in more subtle, sophisticated ways. When we do, it can only lead to unnecessary upset and anxiety.

5. **Unhappiness is the result of external events and happenings that are forced on us and that we have no control over.** Actually 99 percent of the unhappiness we experience is not caused by the unpleasant aspects of real life events but is created internally by the things we say to ourselves about those events. We can control the external events to some extent, and we can learn to control our internal responses to these events almost completely. For example, if I lose my wallet with $50 cash in it I may become very anxious, depressed, and unhappy about it. However, the actual event is *not* that bad. It will take me maybe an hour to notify my credit card companies and the various governmental agencies. I will have to buy a new wallet, and I lost $50. Viewed in terms of a lifetime, the loss of the money and time are, in fact, very small. However, by overreacting, I make it worse and exaggerate its significance. We actually defeat ourselves by our internal reactions. The external event, if viewed rationally, would be a matter of little or no concern. We can often see the truth of this when someone else is involved. We often say, "I wish I had his problems" or "I wish that were my main problem." We also need to see the truth of it in our own experience.

6. **We should be greatly concerned about dangerous and fearful things and must center our thinking on them until the danger is passed.** This is irrational because such thinking will not prevent the thing from happening. In some cases, it even makes it more likely to happen. In other cases, we become so exhausted from worrying that, when it happens, we are less able to cope than if we had not worried so much. Also, the large majority of what we worry about never occurs, or if it does, is not as bad as we expected. The best thing to do is face such situations head-on. One should strive to make them nondangerous and to handle them successfully when they happen, but excessive worrying about them serves no purpose. Even if the worst occurs, we should regard it realistically as an unpleasant event, one that we didn't like, and go on from there. We

need to stop telling ourselves that every problem is a terrible thing and that it is the precursor of the end of the world. It is not.

7. It is easier to avoid difficulties and responsibilities in life than to face them. When we try to avoid difficulties and responsibilities, we only create more and worse problems in the future. It is best to face problems squarely and to solve them to the best of our ability. Putting them off only increases anxiety, depression, and guilt. Facing them increases our feelings of self-confidence, self-esteem, and happiness. The enjoyable life is not one without problems; it is one where we solve problems successfully.

8. We need someone or something stronger than ourselves to rely on. Nobody is completely independent, and we should have no fear of being dependent on others to some extent, as they are on us. However, we should realize that this dependency is a matter of all human beings needing others. It is not so specific that we must have one certain person to be dependent on. If one person fails us or is unavailable, there are other people who can help. Our whole life is never dependent on one other person. Sometimes we may think it is, but it isn't. Life goes on with or without any one individual. On the other side of the coin, we need to develop our own integrity, independence, individuality, and self-expression so that the failure or loss of someone close to us is not devastating.

Being overly dependent on another robs both us and them of the best in life. We become insecure and fail to learn and to grow. They are, in turn, burdened with us and cannot reach their full potential.

A part of this dependency is often expressed as a feeling that people owe us things because we did something for them once or that we are obligated to them for something they did. Neither of these is true. If we want to do something for someone, we should do it, and there should be no strings attached. We should expect nothing in return, except the gratification that we did what we wanted to. Likewise we should not feel obligated to others under similar circumstances. It is stupid and irrational to suffer anguish because somebody returns nothing, or even ill, for our kindness. This does not preclude, of course, striking a clear bargain where the terms are stipulated and understood by each party at the time. We do "give to get" on occasion. However, we also should give a lot just because we want to give, expecting nothing in return. If we do, we'll get our share, in the long run.

9. **Because something greatly influenced us in the past, it must determine our present behavior; the influence of the past cannot be overcome.** This is not true at all. While it is often difficult to change previous learnings, it is not impossible. The essence of life is growth and development. We never stop changing. We are not the same person we were ten years ago. The world and our circumstances are not the same either. We need to learn from past experiences but not be overly attached to them. What may have been necessary and appropriate in the past may not fit or work at all in the present. The rational person develops and improves himself throughout his life.

10. **What other people do is vitally important to us, and we should make every effort to change them to be the way we think they should be.** Actually other people's lives, problems, and behavior are their own business and generally no concern of ours. We really cannot control or change them very much. Efforts to do so backfire more often than not and only serve to worsen the situation. In general, we should strive for the utmost tolerance: to live and let live. Actually we are generally more upset by the implications or interpretations we think are involved in their behavior than by the behavior itself. Usually the supposed implications and interpretations are not in the other person's mind at all. If the other person asks us for help and we want to give assistance, we may. However, we have no reason to force our "help" on those who don't want it. If their behavior directly affects us, we may want to discuss it with them and seek a solution. However, many times we may just have to learn to live with the situation. A professor of psychology in my freshman year at college used to repeat in his lectures, "We may as well learn that people have faults and decide to live with them anyhow."

11. **There is one perfect solution to every problem, and if it is not found, the result will be terrible.** This is irrational because there are many possible solutions to most problems, but seldom is

there any perfect solution. Each alternative solution has some good and some bad features. All we can really do is select one of the better alternatives and give it a try. If it doesn't work, we must try another. We live by doing the best we can in any set of circumstances. When we do this consistently, things seem to go well and catastrophies do not really beset us on every side. To hold out for perfection only causes needless anguish and often leads to worse solutions in the long run. If we hold out for perfection, decisions are often made by default. Seldom are these the best ones.

12. One has virtually no control over his emotions, he is their victim and cannot help how he feels. In reality, we can exert a great amount of control over our feelings in many ways. If we work at it, especially through rational thinking, we can learn to control our emotions rather than being controlled by them.

Thinking about the above types of irrational thinking and employing the alternative principles of rational thinking protects us from much irrational, needless anxiety. Some people have found it helpful to get together with a friend or a group of friends and go over the principles of irrational and rational thinking together. Each can share experiences and examples of the principles and encourage the others to think and live rationally. As the reader may have noted, many of the rational principles are drawn from Stoic philosophy. Those interested may want to read more of the Stoic philosophers. Some of Dr. Ellis's books are also very helpful, such as *A Guide to Rational Living* and *Growth through Reason.*

chapter five

EXISTENTIAL ANXIETY
AND
CREATIVE LIVING

It is almost trite to comment on the rapid tempo of change in society today and on the growth of knowledge, technology, and affluence, but the fact is that the pace has quickened in the last generation or two. As someone has quipped, "If it works, it's obsolete." The world is literally changing so rapidly that children today are born into a world that will no longer exist when they are adults. They will be educated in school for tasks that will no longer have to be done shortly after they graduate. In years gone by, things were more stable and predictable. The struggle for survival seemed to give intrinsic meaning to life and goals seemed obvious. However, with the technology and affluence of today, mere survival is no longer much of a struggle for most people. In such circumstances, people begin to take stock of the meaning and *quality* of their existence. When they do, they often find themselves completely perplexed by questions such as, "Who am I? Where am I going? Why? What does it all mean? Does it really matter?" Intense anxiety and much anguish often accompany these questions.

Some psychotherapists have developed what is called existential psychotherapy to help people deal with these questions and problems. One of the more interesting pioneers in this field is the Viennese psychiatrist Viktor Frankl. Dr. Frankl sometimes asks a despairing patient, "Why is it that you do not commit suicide?"

With that jolting thought, he is able to find a small corner to begin helping the patient find the meaning of his life.

Frankl is well qualified to comment on the meaning of life. His ideas were tested when he was a prisoner in a German concentration camp during World War II. One of his early books was entitled *From Death Camp to Existentialism* (later revised and published as *Man's Search for Meaning*), and it led some people to think he originated his ideas in the camp. However he once told me that he had developed his ideas and had a manuscript for a book describing them before he was taken to the prison camp. His ideas were tested in the camp and he emerged more convinced than ever.

Frankl believes that the main motivation of man is to discover the meaning of his existence. He refers to this as the "will-to-meaning" and contrasts it with the two other prevalent notions about the nature and motivation of man. One is that man is motivated by seeking pleasure and avoiding pain. The hedonistic view is termed by Frankl the "will-to-pleasure." It is endorsed by many in different fields. In psychiatry, Sigmund Freud was one of the main exponents. The second is the idea that man is driven by his desire to master and conquer. This view was proposed by Alfred Adler among others and is characterized by Frankl as the "will-to-power." Frankl thinks that these latter views, while containing a grain of truth, are misconceptions if we are seeking the main motivating force in man. The main force is the drive to understand the meaning of existence. This is what separates man from other animals. The animal seeks pleasure and conquest, but meaning is unknown to him. The essence of man is meaning.

When man's will-to-meaning is frustrated, Frankl refers to this as "existential frustration." This existential frustration grows out of an "existential vacuum" in the person's life and manifests itself mainly in a state of boredom. There is a feeling of emptiness, a void within oneself, and the feeling that nothing is worthwhile. This state of boredom and void is not a mental illness in and of itself. It is a "dis-ease" of the spirit and is common to all men until they resolve it by discovering meaning in their existence. However, if it persists, it is a fertile breeding ground for anxiety, neuroses, and other emotional problems.

Neuroses and emotional disturbances can, of course, arise from other causes, but today a large number of them develop out of existential vacuum and frustration. These are referred to by Frankl as "noögenic neuroses." This word is made up of the word *noos*, which, in this context, means "spirit," "soul," or "mind" and *genic* which refers to "origin" or "beginning." They are neuroses that develop out of the problems of the spirit. Even the other neuroses have an existential dimension in that they involve the spiritual dimension in one way or another. According to Frankl, man cannot make his life meaningful nor can anyone else give him meaning for his life. He must discover it. Others can help with this discovery. Frankl calls the system of psychotherapy that he has developed to do this logotherapy. In this context, *logo* or *logos* refers to "meaning." The treatment helps the person to discover meaning. Frankl is fond of quoting Nietzsche to the effect that he who has a *why* to live for can bear almost any *how*.

Many of the ideas and techniques that Frankl has developed can be used to help deal with the anxieties we often feel in life. Frankl points out that basic to being human is being conscious of and faithful to our responsibilities in life. Living our lives in such a way that we are responsible toward ourselves and toward others is the meaningful life. This is an ongoing process, not a status that we reach. Man is not content when he reaches homeostasis or equilibrium, where all pressures are absent. He is most content or happy, and his life is most meaningful, when he is responsibly meeting and solving problems.

Life also has meaning when one is growing and progressing toward the achievement of values. There are three main areas of these values: creative, experiential, and attitudinal.

Creative values are realized when one works for the benefit of society. When we think of creative contributions to mankind, we generally think of such things as art, music, and literature. These are included in what Frankl means. A person seeking to realize such values might want to take up one of these endeavors as a pastime or a profession. Most community colleges have courses that can get one started in them. The library, of course, has a wealth of information on such areas. There are also individuals and clubs in every community that would facilitate a person's becoming creative in everything from painting to wine making or woodworking. Such achievement provides part of the meaning of life. However, the concept is much broader than this. For example, doing a good job at our work and being proud of our product, whatever it may be, is another way. If we approach our daily jobs as a vehicle for expressing the creative values in life rather than putting in time to get a paycheck, we will discover a real and exciting dimension of existence that is all too often missed in the zombie-like work world we often experience. When we approach our work in such a manner, everyone profits. We have richer lives and we enrich the existence of those around us.

But, the concept is even broader than this. We can give of ourselves to others—friends, family, and neighbors. Putting a bandaid on a child's skinned knee and comforting him is a very creative act. Working in community projects can also be. In responsible achievement, we find one of life's real meanings.

The second area is that of *experiential values*. This has to do with simply experiencing and appreciating such things as love, joy, curiosity, knowledge, nature, music, art, and history. Seeing the Good, the True, the Beautiful, the Interesting, and the Exciting in life leads to the discovery of depth and meaning. We do this by going to places where things are happening and becoming a part. We can attend concerts, visit art galleries, go to plays. Athletic events, if properly viewed, are a thrilling art form. Travel, reading, and a host of other activities could be included. There is an old joke about the man who spent a month one weekend in Waco, Texas. However for a person who experiences and appreciates life, such a weekend could be an exciting adventure. Experiential values can also be realized by knowing a person in all of his uniqueness. Talking with and getting to know other human beings can be a remarkable experience if real communication occurs.

Attitudinal values have to do with facing life with the right attitudes. For example, if we can avoid suffering, we should; however if we are faced with unavoidable suffering, this can be a positive force in our lives. Suffering is ennobling if it is for a purpose, and we bear up under it with strength. If our suffering contributes to another person or to an important cause, we are privileged to bear it. In one of his writings, Frankl tells of an old man who was despondent because his wife, whom he loved very much, had died. Frankl told the man that he was very happy for him. The man replied, "How can you say that?" Frankl went on to point out to him that if he had died first, his wife would have known the grief. However, since she died first, he was privileged to bear the grief for her.

We also learn from suffering. Tribulation is a great instructor. The carefree life may be good, but the lessons of suffering lead to a personality of much greater depth and quality. Suffering can be a strong stimulus to growth and development. Thus, real meaning in life can often be found in suffering.

Another attitudinal value has to do with one's view of happiness. Frankl has characterized the United States as being afflicted by "fun morality." We feel that the basic value and goal in life is to be happy and have fun. This robs us of the significance of suffering in life because when we suffer we feel doubly bad. We feel bad because of the suffering, and also we feel ashamed and bad because of our unhappiness. However, the right attitude toward happiness is that it is not to be sought after, or even expected, all of the time. It is a by-product of living our lives in such a way that we fulfill their meaning and attain positive values. This is true happiness as opposed to fun.

Another attitudinal value concerns time. In his book *The Doctor and the Soul* (New York: Alfred A. Knopf, 1972, 2nd ed., pp. 33–34) Frankl includes the following comments on time:

> Time that has passed is certainly irrecoverable; but, what has happened within that time is unassailable and inviolable. Passing time is therefore not only a thief, but a trustee. Any philosophy which keeps in mind the transitoriness of existence need not be at all pessimistic. To express this point figuratively we might say: The pessimist resembles a man who observes with fear and sadness that his wall calendar, from which he daily tears a sheet, grows thinner with each passing day. On the other hand, the person who takes life in the sense suggested above is like a man who removes each successive leaf from his calendar and files it neatly and carefully

away with its predecessors—after first having jotted a few diary notes on the back. He can reflect with pride and joy on all the richness set down in these notes, on all the life he has already lived to the full. What will it matter to him if he notices that he is growing old? Has he any reason to envy the young people whom he sees, or wax nostalgic for his own youth? What reasons has he to envy a young person? For the *possibilities* that a young person has, the future that is in store for him? "No, thank you," he will think. "Instead of possibilities, I have realities in my past—not only the reality of work done, but of love loved and of suffering suffered. These are the things of which I am most proud—though these are things which cannot inspire envy."

One's attitude toward his role in life is similarly important. Everyone has a unique destiny and contribution to make in life that nobody else can make for him. It is his responsibility to find that role and his duty to carry it out. Doing so gives meaning to life. Death also gives meaning rather than destroying it. If life were not finite, everything could be put off until later. There would be no need for us to be active, to do, to accomplish. The fact that life must end makes the present significant. Thus, death is a part of life. It is sometimes interesting to approach a new day as though one were living it for the second time and had done it wrong the first time as he might this time, had he not thought about it in this new way.

Living a life that expresses itself in the ways outlined above results in a life that has meaning. The person does not experience needless anxiety because of existential frustration.

There are also some specific techniques that Frankl has developed that he uses with his patients. These techniques enable the person to put things in perspective and discover the meaning in their lives. One is called paradoxical intention.

Paradoxical intention is based on the theory that in many cases maladaptive behavior develops because the person is literally afraid of fear, that is, he thinks a certain situation will make him anxious and then becomes extremely frightened even about getting into the situation. This is called anticipatory anxiety and it can build up to disabling proportions. The fear of being frightened by the situation, as well as the fear of the situation, develops into a vicious circle that makes one avoid the situation as vigorously as possible and renders him overwhelmed with anxiety so that he is almost unable to function if he is forced into the situation.

In using paradoxical intention in such a situation, the person is told to try to do the thing he fears most in the situation or to wish for the thing to happen. This, of course, is paradoxical. The pathogenic fear is replaced by a paradoxical wish. This technique takes the wind out of the sails of anticipatory anxiety, enabling the person to relax and handle the situation much more calmly. A humorous example of this is offered by Frankl. He tells the story of a very severe stutterer he treated as an adult. The man told him he had stuttered ever since he could remember. There was only one occasion when he didn't; it was when he was twelve years old. He hooked a ride on a streetcar and was caught by the conductor. He thought to himself that he would stutter and show the conductor that he was just a poor stuttering child. But when he tried to stutter, he was unable to do so.

Another example, from one of Frankl's colleagues, concerns a man who had had a heart attack. He became very afraid of any sign of change in the rate of his heartbeat and was afraid to leave the hospital for fear that he might need medical attention at any moment of the day. When one of his anxiety attacks started, he was told to make his heart beat faster, increase the pain, and get as anxious as possible. The nurse then left him alone for awhile. When she returned, he said he couldn't do it. In fact, the opposite happened. He now felt calm. This encouraged him enough to get up and take a walk outside the hospital, something he had not done for six months. In one of the shops he started to feel his heart beat faster. He started saying to himself, "Try to feel even more anxiety." Again, he couldn't do it and actually became calmer. Soon after, he went home and returned to his job.

If a person wanted to use this technique for fear of public speaking, he might say to himself just before getting up to speak, "I'm going to get as anxious as possible. I want anxiety and stage fright to flow through and envelop my whole body. I want to tremble and quake; to perspire and turn red; to stammer and stutter. I will be so anxious the whole building will tremble with me, and I'll probably drown the audience in perspiration. One thing is for sure, if the water doesn't get them, the smell will. I'll be the world's champion. Number One in stage fright. Do they have an Olympic category for that? I will have the gold medal." Doing this will, paradoxically, make you calmer. It is important to ridicule the fear and to use a sense of humor in deciding what you will say to yourself about the fear. This defuses the situation, making it possible for you to function quite effectively.

According to Frankl, the way this fits into a theory based on discovering the meaning of life is that it calls attention to the way we often focus our attention on the trivial things in life and exaggerate them all out of proportion. This leads to irrational, unnecessary anxiety. If we call a halt to such nonsense and begin to concentrate on more meaningful things, we get rid of anxieties and live a more fulfilling, more purposeful, and happier life. Paradoxical intention is a way of calling the bluff on these trivial fears. Of course, such fears thrive in an existential vacuum. So living a meaningful life is good protection from them.

Another technique developed by Frankl is called de-reflection. De-reflection is somewhat similar to paradoxical intention. It is intended to counteract the obsessive-compulsive tendency we often develop toward self-observation. We often begin to pay too much attention to something. The more we think and ruminate about it, the worse the situation becomes. A good example is breathing. Try to watch your breathing and breathe normally. The more you try, the more your breathing becomes arhythmical; the harder you try, the worse it gets. The same is true for insomnia. If you try to force yourself to go to sleep, you only insure that you will stay awake. In the morning, when you give up because you have to get up, you fall asleep. It is possible to try too hard at some things, making success less likely than if we took it easier. In de-reflection the person is told simply to ignore the problem. Of course, many times this is easier said than done. However, it helps if we redirect our attention from the thing that is troubling us to some more meaningful value or something of importance. Once we do this, we often find that this resolves the problem. It no longer causes us undue anxiety.

Frankl contrasts the right and wrong approach concerning

situations where these techniques are appropriate by talking about right and wrong passivity as well as right and wrong activity.

Wrong passivity refers to withdrawal from situations as a result of anticipatory anxiety. It is a flight from fear. Right passivity is the use of paradoxical intention. Through this technique, the person stops fighting the situation, but is able to become involved in it without fear or anxiety.

Wrong activity is obsessively and compulsively dwelling on a problem or a concern until we are trying too hard and the goal becomes unattainable because of our overeffort. De-reflection is the right kind of activity in this situation. The person ignores the problem and redirects his attention to more important things.

chapter six

LIFE STRUCTURING
AND
ENGINEERING

Often a lack of planning of our lives and the tasks we must accomplish results in our being subjected to many little tensions, anxieties, and hassles that are unnecessary and can be avoided very easily. Planning may be thought of as structuring or engineering. In structuring, we give organization to situations and set things up so that they will go smoothly. In engineering a situation, we develop a plan or a strategy of activity that will lead to a desired result.

Let's consider structuring first. Many times we are confronted with a task that puzzles us in terms of exactly how we should proceed. We don't know where or how to start. This leads to much anxiety and frustration. Often it results in our putting off doing anything about the task and eventually leads to failure. Frequently, if we can just clearly structure the situation, we will get over the hump of inactivity. Then we have a good chance of successfully completing the task. For example, suppose our boss says he wants us to give a talk to a group of new employees at a dinner meeting. This is a rather vague request, and in many companies, it might be communicated to a person over the phone or in a memo following a meeting by the committee planning the program. Such a vague request often leads to considerable anxiety about what is expected and what to say. We want to do a good job, especially in front of so many people, but we really don't know where to start. However, if we structure the situation carefully, the task becomes much easier. To structure the situation, we might tell the person making the request that we need a little more information in order to make plans. We would then ask a number of questions such as, "What will have been covered in earlier meetings with the employees? What function is the talk to fulfill? How long should it be? Should it be light and entertaining or a more hard-hitting 'pep talk'? Are there any points that should definitely be covered, or is the content entirely open? Are there any copies of talks given in previous meetings?" Once answers to questions of this type are obtained, the task becomes more manageable. The simple technique of structuring the situation keeps us from floundering and gets us started in the right direction.

It is also important to consider similar structuring questions about tasks we assign ourselves. If we think about what it is we are trying to accomplish, it will often help amazingly in our efficient carrying out of the task without undue anxiety and frustration. The basic principle of *structuring* applies to all sorts of tasks. Take, for example, a minor repair job around the house. If we think about what has to be done, plan a little, and see that we have the correct tools and materials at hand, the job can be fun. It is often enjoyable to putter around at little tasks. However, poor structuring results in such experiences ending in frustration, anger, and failure.

Another very simple example might be routine tasks that we must do every day. For example, many people lay out their clothes for the next day before they go to bed. They can sleep peacefully and when they wake up in the morning, they can get dressed and ready without having to make a lot of decisions or having to look for articles of clothing. I myself find it helpful to put things under my car keys if I don't want to forget them. That way, I can't leave without seeing them. These are very simple things, but they can greatly reduce the number of daily hassles we get involved in.

Another common structuring technique that some people use is to keep track of appointments and duties by writing them on a calendar marked with the hours of the day every day of the year. Calendars of this type are made small enough to carry in a vest pocket or to keep on a desk. Keeping such a book around the house or office helps people structure their days and enables them to keep track of things. Other people find such a system too constraining. I myself fail to write everything down and keep forgetting to look at the calendar until it is too late, and I have missed several appointments. People like me find it works better to jot things down on small pieces of paper. I constantly make lists of things to do and write notes to myself about things I want to remember. I try to keep small pieces of paper handy at all times. They are on my desk, by my chair at home, in my wallet, by the bed, in my brief case, etc. When I need to make a note or a list, I grab one of these and write on it. I then clip them together and leave them where I will see them. I may put them in my pockets, in my shoes (so I'll see them in the morning), in my wallet (so I'll be reminded when I buy something), on my desk, and in similar places. Periodically, I sort through my papers, threw the old ones away, put the imminent ones on top, revise some, etc. People are often amused at my "system." It is messy, but it works for me, and that is what is important. I virtually never miss a meeting or an appointment.

I remember reading about a professor who also used this system. Eventually, his students caught on, and as a joke they began to write nonsense notes which they put in his pockets and on his desk when he wasn't looking. The old gentleman spent considerable time trying to figure out what he had meant when he wrote those notes.

There are many other small structuring techniques that can make life more comfortable. Scheduling your departure for meetings and appointments with enough time so that you don't have to rush is an example. Of course, it is possible to get overly anxious about being on time. This is a mistake too. It is best, however, to start out early enough to make it on time and establish a reputation for being punctual. Then, if on occasion, you are late, you can take your time and not worry about it. Since you are usually on time, being a little late sometimes is easily forgiven.

While one can become overly compulsive about such techniques, life structuring can prevent many needless anxieties from ever arising. Thinking and planning in advance are the keys. If we do that well, the event will be no problem when it occurs. Often when I'm coaching a student about a public presentation he is going to make, I tell him to be sure to have a closing sentence in mind for his talk. Otherwise, he may get to the end and discover he has no way to stop. The feeling of panic and growing embarrassment that develops as a public speaker in this situation continues to talk without making any further sense can easily be avoided by planning the closing in advance. The same principle applies to many other areas of life. Planning and structuring prevent anxiety.

As we indicated at the outset, engineering of life situations is also very important in reducing anxiety. Engineering involves a more active process than structuring. There are many situations which are very frustrating and cause significant anxiety. However with some forethought it is often possible to engineer the problems out of the situation. A good example of this concerns the common problem of Sunday neurosis. Many people find their week very hectic and look forward to the relaxation of the weekend. Often, the weekend starts out all right and they do feel relief. However, by Sunday afternoon they begin to feel depressed, anxious, and at loose ends. They just don't know what to do with themselves and feel miserable. They find themselves desperately wishing it was Monday morning so they could go back to work and get over their distress. This is, of course, very unfortunate because Sunday afternoon and evening can be a very enjoyable time. Most people do not relax nearly enough, and this opportunity should not be wasted.

A very effective way to deal with a Sunday neurosis is to engineer it out of existence. The way to do this is simple. Plan some activity that you ordinarily enjoy but don't get around to doing very often and do it during that time. Take the family for a ride. Go to the beach. Go on a picnic. Invite some friends over to watch a football game or for dinner. Work on a hobby. Go to a concert. See a movie. Visit relatives. There are a thousand things that can be done. Doing these will make the week more enjoyable because you can look forward to them. It will make the weekend more enjoyable by helping you to relax and have some pleasant recreation. Make sure the activity selected is one that is relaxing, that you sincerely enjoy, and that adds a pleasant dimension to your life. Usually, if one does this for a few weeks, the problem of Sunday neurosis disappears. At that point, it is not necessary to plan some major activity every

Sunday, but occasional activities will continue to be very enjoyable.

Of course, if we frequently feel the effects of rather intense Sunday neuroses, and if our attempts at engineering do not prove very successful, it may be that there are some unresolved problems in our lives that we crowd out by keeping busy during the week. When we finally slow down, these problems hit us and the feelings are depressing. If this is the case, it is wise to think about and work out solutions to these problems either on our own or with help from a friend or a professional counselor. However, many times Sunday neuroses are not that deep or complicated.

Another example of engineering can be found in the area of entertaining. Most people are fairly adept at this and do a good job at engineering this rather simple situation. However, many others have problems with it and become very anxious when called on to entertain guests in their home. Even those who do not have much trouble in this area may have trouble if the guests are unusually important or threatening in some way. Proper engineering in this type of situation calls for deciding what type of entertaining you wish to do. Is it to be a large cocktail party or a small, intimate dinner party? Will it be for old friends or for people who have not previously met? Once some basic decisions of this sort are made, you can begin to engineer the situation so that anxiety will be unlikely to occur. You need to consider the evening from start to finish and arrange things so they will go smoothly. For example, if it is to be a small dinner party, you may already know whether any of the guests have specific dietary requirements due to health problems or strong personal likes or dislikes. If you do not know, it is a good idea to check this with each guest. With this information, it will be possible to plan a menu. The menu might be one that involves food that is not highly risky in terms of the possibility of turning out badly and that can be prepared to a considerable extent ahead of time. The guests should be chosen so that they will enjoy each other's company and will be able to keep a lively conversation going. Structured activities such as listening to one of the guests sing or play a musical instrument can be planned to add to the evening.

While the above are only sketchy examples, planning of this type will have the effect of engineering anxiety out of such situations. It is better to engineer situations in this manner and keep anxiety from growing out of proportion than to avoid them or to endure them with great pain. After we have had some successful experiences, the planning and engineering will not need to be so elaborate. Much of it will become implicit, and we won't even have to think about it.

The same general point can be made about all of the suggestions made in this chapter. They may seem rather elaborate and overdrawn. But, the point is that they should be used to reduce anxiety and hassles in situations that often upset us. If we don't need them in certain situations, then no purpose is served by using them.

We all have situations that just seem to be hard for us to handle. Structuring and engineering can often make them easier to manage. The exact situations that need that type of planning and the specific techniques used will vary from person to person depending on his own life style, what seems to work for him, and what he is comfortable with, but anxiety can be planned out of existence with proper structuring and engineering.

chapter seven

REALISTIC GOAL SETTING

Some people just drift along with the tide. They don't seem to have any goals. Their lives appear to lack direction. As a result, they don't achieve much. Often they are very capable and talented individuals. People who know them frequently lament the tragedy that they are not more goal directed and more productive.

At the other extreme are people who constantly set very high goals for themselves. In fact they set such high goals that it is impossible to achieve them. These people are chronically tense and miserable because they are constantly failing. Every unachieved goal is a failure. Even goals that they achieve but which took longer to achieve than they had planned are regarded as failures. Such people drive themselves relentlessly. Often they accomplish a great deal, but they don't enjoy it. The fact that they didn't accomplish as much as they had wanted to as soon as they had hoped robs them of any pleasure in their achievement. After a time they find their energy sapped by this tension. They become disillusioned with their goals and frequently turn to cynicism and depression.

Both of the above types of individual suffer from the same basic problem. They are unable to formulate realistic goals to guide their lives. Commonly the one who drifts with the tide either sets very low goals or does not set goals at all because of fear and anxiety. He is afraid he will fail and knows that that will make him anxious;

therefore, he does not set goals. The second type of person sets goals that are too high. As we saw above, this also results in defeat.

In addition to goals being too high or too low, we can set false goals for ourselves. This, likewise, leads to disaster. When we do this, we find ourselves expending a great deal of energy and time to achieve something, only to find that it was not what we wanted at all. Sometimes it is not possible to detect false goals in advance, but often if we examine our values and think about the goal, we can determine whether or not we really want it. When couples come to me for marriage counseling, the subject of divorce frequently arises. Many times the partners are sure that they want a divorce. They think they could be happy if only they could get rid of their lousy partner. I ask them to think about it a bit and tell me how many things actually would be different and in what ways they would be different if they were no longer married to their partner. Sometimes, when they do this, they realize that they have been *blaming* their partner for everything unpleasant in their lives, but if they are honest, they realize that the real causes lie elsewhere. Divorce, in such cases, is a false goal; in other cases, of course, it may be a very legitimate goal.

The task is to set good, realistic goals for ourselves. If we do so, it gives direction to our lives, gives us a feeling of accomplishment when we achieve the goals, and helps us be successful, productive people.

To better understand the process of setting goals we need to understand that there are long-range and short-range goals. Long-range goals refer to major things we want to accomplish eventually in our lives. Short-range goals refer to the things we have to do more or less immediately: they are the tasks that we set for ourselves to accomplish each day. Long-range goals are generally achieved by accomplishing many short-range goals. For example, if we want to be a teacher in high school, this is a long-range goal. Short-range goals toward that end would include passing tests and completing assignments in the necessary courses in college, accumulating a sufficient number of credit hours, obtaining our college degree, and finding a job.

There are rules which when followed enable one to get good long-

and short-range goals. The following rules apply to setting long-range goals. First, decide whether the goal is an appropriate one or not. Watch out for those that are too high, too low, or possibly false. Careful consideration of all relevant information will serve as a guide. It also helps to talk to others and learn from their experience. Get good advice from friends and/or professionals about whether this is a good, realistic goal for a person such as you. In the end, however, you will have to make the decision.

Second, make long-range goals that are general rather than specific. If they are too specific, we almost always set ourselves up for failure. If they are more general, we will find that they can be achieved in a number of ways, and we can be content with a number of accomplishments. It is better to set the goal of being an educated person and going as far as circumstances permit in college training, than to make the goal obtaining a Ph.D. from Harvard with a straight A average. It is better to set a goal of being a good contributor to community betterment than to decide that we must be voted the most outstanding citizen by some club and be elected the youngest mayor the city ever had. Goals that are too specific almost always are frustrated and lead to a feeling of failure. Even when achieved, they are often found to be hollow and false.

Third, once a long-range goal is selected, carefully analyze it in terms of the exact short-range goals that must be accomplished to get there. Determine the path of short-range subgoals that is most likely to lead successfully to the long-range goal *for you.* There is almost always more than one way to achieve a given long-range goal. You don't have to do it the way somebody else did. You need to go about it the way that is most likely to lead to success for you, with your strengths, weaknesses, and personality. That's how the Fosbury Flop came into being.

Fourth, start working systematically on the short-range goals and *be patient.* Things that are worthwhile take time. Set up a time schedule that is realistic. Then, allow yourself half again that amount of time before you begin to worry about not making progress. People with goals they want to achieve always underestimate the length of time it will take to accomplish them. This sentiment is expressed in the humorous retort to the old saying,

"Rome wasn't built in a day, you know." The retort is "Yes, but I wasn't foreman on that job." Things always seem to go slower than you had hoped. I remember one of my research assistants telling me one day that he had discovered a basic principle of research. I asked him what it was. He replied, "Things take longer than they do." The point is we must be patient with goals. Otherwise we set ourselves up for chronic frustration, tension, and anxiety.

The following rules are helpful in setting short-range goals. First, as with long-range goals, short-range goals should be realistic. They should be small and discrete steps toward the long-range goal. They should be things we can do more or less immediately and that will move us along toward the long-range goal.

Second, they should be more specific than the long-range goals. They should be sufficiently specific to enable us to know what we want to accomplish next and where we are going. Otherwise we will find ourselves standing around thinking that we want to get closer to our long-range goal but making no progress in the right direction.

Third, our approach to accomplishing these short-range goals should be planned and organized in such a way that we have a high likelihood of getting them done. The ideas presented in chapter six can be put to work here.

Fourth, if we fail at one of our short-range goals, we should not make more of it than it really is. We often catastrophize at times like this and behave as though one false step means we will never make it to our ultimate goal. This is rarely, if ever, the case. If we fail at a short-range goal, we should back up and try it again, or we should figure out an alternate route that will get us around the barrier. We should not let minor setbacks depress us. They are to be *expected* and *overcome*. They are all part of it.

When you achieve a short-range goal, celebrate it. Celebrate liberally as you go along. Psychologists would refer to this as reinforcement or rewarding yourself for desired behavior. Whatever you call it, it is very effective. The "celebration" can be a small thing or something bigger. For example, if a person is studying for an exam, he can put some nuts or candy or a soft drink on the table. The material to be studied can then be divided into very small units, such as pages, sections of chapters, or basic concepts. As each unit is completed, you can reward yourself with a piece of candy or a sip of the soft drink. It is important to keep the study units small and reward yourself with small amounts of the candy or drink frequently. Massive rewards after massive amounts of work are less successful. If you try this, you will find that studying goes a lot faster and is much more enjoyable. This basic idea can be applied to all sorts of tasks. It is a simple technique, but you will be amazed at how effectively it works.

Of course the celebration can also be more major for accomplishing a more major short-range goal or for the final accomplishment of a long-range goal. Thus completion of a course or a semester might call for dinner at an expensive restaurant, a short vacation trip, or a gift for ourselves. Use of this approach makes getting there half the fun. People who arrange their lives this way enjoy themselves and what they are doing.

Once the long-range and short-range goals have been considered and established, it is best to shift our attention and emphasis to *process*. The goals have to be carried lightly. If we fix our attention on them too firmly, we will find ourselves too future oriented to ever enjoy the present—always going somewhere but never arriving. Looking forward too much to goals in the future leads us to be unhappy with the present moment and to make excessive sacrifices to get to our goals. However, when we get to those goals, we always establish new ones and begin the process over. In that way we never enjoy living in the present, because we are preparing to enjoy the future, and that future never comes. Goals are for direction and planning. After they have been established, we need to put them in the back of our mind and begin to concentrate on process. Concentrating on process means immersing ourselves in and thoroughly enjoying what we are doing now, not just as a means to an end but as an experience in and of itself. If we have our direction set by goals and throw ourselves wholeheartedly into the process of living and doing, we are most likely to enjoy our lives and achieve our goals. As in many areas of life, we can go too far in either extreme. It is the right balance which is most satisfying.

Of course, saying we are not going to think about our goals too much is easier than actually doing so. In order to keep the goals and process in perspective we need to be mentally vigilant and refuse to let ourselves become preoccupied with future goals. We can do this by working at being patient and by forcing ourselves not to think about them too much. If you have trouble doing this, there is a technique called thought stopping which might help.

Thought stopping is an anxiety-reducing technique that is used to get rid of obsessive ideas or thoughts that sometimes incessantly run through a person's mind. Often these thoughts preoccupy a person to such an extent that he can't seem to get them out of his mind. This can be very upsetting and anxiety producing. In using the thought-stopping technique, the patient is instructed to get the thought that has been bothering him firmly in mind. He then signals to the therapist, who shouts very loudly, "Stop! Stop! Stop!" This is repeated several times each session for two or three sessions. After a few times, the patient is instructed to say "Stop" in his mind while the therapist says it out loud. Then he is told to say it in his mind when the thought comes to him during the day. He is also instructed that after he shouts "Stop" in his mind he should think of something or do something else that will absorb his interest. This rather simple technique is often very effective in ridding a person of obsessive thoughts. If you have this problem in any area, you might want to give it a try. You, of course, could use it to reduce preoccupation with goals. Simply have a friend play the part of the therapist and shout "Stop" for you. Often, if the thought is only mildly obsessive, you can skip the part of having someone shout, "Stop." You can just say it emphatically to yourself in your mind and then say, "I'm not going to think about that now." Following this, think about or do something else.

Another technique that often works in helping us to keep from being obsessively preoccupied with goals is to write them down on a piece of paper or in a notebook. Just writing them down reassures us that they won't be forgotten and we need not be mentally vigilant about them anymore in terms of keeping them in our mind. Having them on paper relieves us of that. Many people get their notebook out from time to time, read over their list of goals, and fantasize or project themselves into the future. They let their minds wander and think about what it will be like when they reach certain goals and the things they will do along the way to achieve them. Such fantasies are useful because they keep us motivated and often serve as a type of planning session. Using such fantasy sessions frees us to think about other things in between.

One final word about goal setting. In setting goals, flexibility is a very important point to keep in mind. Goals, once set, should not be looked on as "musts." With time, circumstances change and we change. What may have been a good goal when originally formulated may not be such a good idea at a later time. Therefore, it is necessary to be flexible and willing to change goals from time to time. This can be done as we go along, day by day. Or, some people use the leisure of vacation time to take a trip and re-evaluate goals when they have more time to really think them through. Sometimes we reach an important point along the way toward a goal that can serve as an occasion to reassess the goal. We may choose to continue on, to change the goal slightly, or even to abandon it in favor of some other goal which now seems better. There is only so much time in life, and we can't do everything we might like to. A friend of mine used to say, "We are what we are at the expense of something we might have been." This fact makes goal setting and periodic goal revision crucial.

chapter eight

ASSERTION

One of the most effective ways to keep anxiety at a minimum in our lives is to deal with problems as they arise, without putting them off. If we put off dealing with problems, often something that would have been easy to handle grows in seriousness and gets out of hand. Nipping things in the bud is a secret of success that many highly successful people have learned to use.

Another aspect of procrastination is that even if the situation does not really become worse, our anxiety about it often increases until what is actually a minor problem becomes a major *psychological* hurdle. In our mind it is a major problem.

If we handle tasks and problems as they come along, it stands to reason that we will have less anxiety in the long run because we will have fewer unsolved problems and increasing tension nagging at us. Also, we will be able to enjoy our other activities and leisure more because we have gotten the problem out of the way. For example, you may have a job to do that takes one hour to complete. It may be that the remainder of the day or evening is free for relaxation. If you do the job first and get it out of the way, you can relax completely with a clear conscience. You have the pleasure of knowing that the job is done. However, if you try to relax first, while planning to do the job later, you often will find that you are unable to relax as completely. The knowledge that the job is not done yet and that you will soon have to do it, keeps you tense.

There is an old saying that the best defense is a good offense. While this is not always true, it works in many situations. Psychologists frequently refer to learning to take action in the right way and at the right time as *assertion training*. The idea behind this is that if we take appropriate positive action, we prevent anxiety from building up. Fear often results from a feeling that we are helpless. Doing something about a problem gives us the feeling of adequacy and success, which is an antidote for the helpless feelings that often accompany anxiety. Any kind of action usually helps somewhat. Appropriate action helps most. Many athletes, performers, and others know that most of their anxiety occurs *before* the game or before they get on stage. Once they get into action, the anxiety leaves. Most of us have had this same experience in one way or another.

I once had a patient who told me that life was a clam. At first I thought this was some kind of delusional statement; however when I asked him to explain, he said, "You have to jump on it and pry it open to get the goodies out." So proper assertion does lead to a more rewarding and anxiety-free life.

Often when we face problems head on, we discover that they were not nearly as bad as we imagined them to be in our anxious ruminations. Norman Vincent Peale tells a story about something that happened on his honeymoon. He and his new wife were alone in a secluded mountain retreat. Dr. Peale happened to hear over the radio that a dangerous killer was on the loose in the area. He immediately began to be afraid that his wife and he might be in danger. After awhile, he heard a sound out in front of their cabin. There were footsteps on the front porch. They stopped in front of the door. Though very frightened, Dr. Peale decided he had to protect himself and his wife. With all the courage he could muster, he went to the door and threw it open. There on the porch was a small chipmunk! If we face them head on, a lot of the killers in our lives turn out to be chipmunks.

Some time ago, my neighbor was taking a trip and asked me to watch his boat while he was gone. Some vandals had been stealing motors from boats in people's yards. One night while he was gone, I looked out the window and saw two men trying to get the motor from my neighbor's boat. Without thinking, I went charging out of the house, pointed a finger at the two, and told them to stop right there. Fortunately, they both got up and ran. After they were gone, it began to dawn on me that I was standing there alone in my pajamas pointing a finger at two men armed with wrenches and hammers. If they had not run, it would not have been much of a contest. The point is that pure, simple assertion will take you a long way. Appropriate assertion is better and will get you farther in the long run. We will talk more about appropriate assertion in the latter part of this chapter.

First, however, it is important to distinguish between assertion and aggression. Assertion is attacking a problem, standing up for our rights, or doing the right thing at the right time. We are simply doing what we believe to be the right thing to do in the situation, and we do it without malice. Aggression applies to a situation where our attack is mixed with hostility and malice. We often realize that we are going too far or are overreacting due to our anger, but we go ahead anyhow. Assertion is a mature, balanced, and fair approach. Aggression, generally, is an immature one that is often not fair.

Perhaps an example will serve to clarify the distinction in the terms we are using here. Suppose somebody does something we don't like. The aggressive response might be to confront him with it in a heated argument and/or look for some way to get revenge. The assertive way would be to approach him and honestly tell him that we didn't like what happened. We might then show a willingness to listen to his side of the story and to discuss ways to prevent the situation from occurring again. It is obvious that the latter approach will usually lead to a happier, less anxious life style.

To develop appropriate assertive behavior as a way of handling problems, it is necessary to analyze the situation very carefully. We must first decide what the proper and appropriate way of handling the situation is. In order to do this, we must be very objective and carefully consider all the possibilities. Often it helps to talk it over with a friend whose judgment we trust. That person can help us think clearly. It is, of course, crucial that we let him know that we want his help and his judgment in determining what is the *appropriate* way to handle the situation. Otherwise he may try to show his friendship by supporting us in whatever we seem to want to do or may suggest some highly idealistic way of looking at the situation that sounds good but that won't work in practice. Once we have decided on the appropriately assertive course of action, we need to plan in detail how we can do it and then go ahead and carry out the plan. It is best to pick some easy situations in which to practice assertion and then tackle more and more difficult ones as we increase our confidence. It is also often best to start with mildly assertive behaviors in situations and increase the strength of the assertion over time. However the important thing is to determine the appropriate assertive response for a given situation, plan exactly how we will do it, and then go ahead and do it. After it is over, we can analyze how it went and, if necessary, revise our plan for the next time.

Let's look at an example of this. Suppose we have a job to do such as figuring our income tax for the year—a task fraught with anxiety and approached with excessive procrastination by many people. We might analyze the situation and decide that it has to be done; there is no way to get out of it. Putting it off until the last possible minute only increases the anxiety and makes it more horrendous in the end. We may then determine to just take the bull by the horns, sit down, and start figuring out our income, deductions, etc. Perhaps we will just work on it an hour the first night. We will then return to the task the next night and the next for similar periods of time until it is done. After we have gotten into the habit of handling tasks in a mildly assertive manner such as this, we may find that we can easily be more strongly assertive in the future. For example, it may not take much time to analyze the situation, and we may find that we can sit down and do the job in one evening instead of spreading it out in small doses for several evenings. By practicing, we can train ourselves to handle situations in an assertive rather than a procrastinating manner.

Or, take another example. Suppose you have a friend who

borrows something of yours, say, a lawnmower, and fails to return it promptly. This causes you a lot of inconvenience because it is not available when you need it. A mild approach to assertion might be to tell him the next time he borrows it that it is fine to borrow the lawnmower and that you don't mind that, but you might go on to tell him that you would like it returned right after he has finished using it. Tell him that you may want to mow your own lawn and want it to be there in case you "take a notion to cut the grass." You can, of course, tell him this pleasantly and with a bit of humor. If you do it right, your friend will not be offended, and you will get your lawnmower back. If he is offended by such a simple, appropriate request, this should be looked on as his problem not yours.

A slightly stronger form of assertion might come later (if he failed to bring the mower back even after your mild attempt at assertion) or if you simply decide that you no longer wish to lend your mower. The stronger form of assertion might be to tell the friend that you have decided not to lend the mower out anymore. You can explain that frequently it is not there when you need it, that it is beginning to show signs of wear, and you don't want to have to put a lot of money into it for repair, etc. You should handle the situation with tact and humor, but stand your ground. It is possible that the person may resent it, but if handled correctly, it is unlikely.

One way to further reduce the possibility of the friend's being offended is to do something that shows you are not rejecting him in turning down his request; you are only setting limits in an area where you think they are needed. The way to show a person he is accepted even though his request is rejected might be to invite him in for a cup of coffee while you talk or invite him to dinner sometime or compliment him for something he has done. In this manner you tell him that you still value his friendship, but you need to put some limits on the situation under discussion. Any reasonable person will be able to accept and understand this.

From the examples above, it can be seen that assertion can be used in simple task-oriented situations and in interpersonal interaction situations. While the examples given are very simple ones, the

64

technique works well in more complex and emotionally charged situations also.

Deciding what is the fair and appropriate thing to do in a situation is crucial in using assertion. After you have determined what it is, do it openly, honestly, and with tact and humor.

A good thing to do after you have asserted yourself is to analyze how it went, so that you can learn how to handle such situations better in the future. Following the analysis, you may want to reinforce or mildly punish yourself for what you did. If you feel you did the right thing, you should say to yourself, "I did what I thought was the right thing to do in that situation. That's good. I'm glad I did that. Maybe I'm wrong, but I did what I sincerely thought was right. That's all anyone has a right to expect." By doing this you reinforce yourself for doing what you did. You feel good and happy about it. If someone disagrees, you might say something like, "Well, I did what I thought was right. Tell me what you think and what you would have done." Then, without becoming anxious or upset, you will be able to discuss the other person's view and possibly get some feedback and information that will help you handle similar situations in the future. You can still rest secure in the knowledge that in the original instance you did what you thought was right, and that is all you can do, it is all anyone can do.

Sometimes mild punishment of ourselves may be in order. If we handled something badly, it does no good to pretend that we didn't. It is best to say something like, "Well, I blew that one. I should have handled it differently." However, the punishment should be *mild.* And, we should philosophically accept the fact that failure is a part of life. The important thing is to learn from our mistakes and failures so that we can do better in the future. Everybody fails sometimes. The successful person is not one who never experiences failure, but one who learns something from each failure.

Often, after we have decided to assert ourselves in a situation, we may have trouble figuring out the best way to do it. Or we may know the best way but doubt our ability to actually carry it out. If we are not sure how to handle it, we can use a technique that psychologists call modeling. It is a basic fact that we learn a lot in life from copying other people. This is what psychologists mean by modeling. We model our behavior by imitating what other people do, as many parents have learned to their chagrin. The same principle applies in athletics. Coaches demonstrate techniques and encourage beginning athletes to watch the professionals use those techniques. Likewise we learn much from friends, teachers, and others just by seeing what they do and trying it ourselves. This can help us learn to be properly assertive. We can observe someone who asserts himself the way we would like to and see how he handles such situations. "You can see a lot just by observing," Yogi Berra once said. Later we can do the same thing in a similar situation that involves us. We may not be too good at it the first time, but with practice we can improve. If we don't have an opportunity to observe our model in all of the situations we want to work in, we can imagine how he would handle it. When possible, it is important to actually observe what our model does in a situation rather than asking him what he would do. The way he says he would handle a situation and the way he would actually handle it may be quite different.

Earlier in this book, we talked about behavior rehearsal, which is practicing behavior before we try it in a given situation. That approach works very well with assertion. We can practice alone, possibly in front of a mirror. Or, we can get someone to play the other part and help us. Practice makes us more skilled and able to behave naturally when the situation calls for it.

Another aid to assertive behavior is reading some of the books on positive thinking. Such books as *The Power of Positive Thinking* by Norman Vincent Peale, *How to Win Friends and Influence People* by Dale Carnegie, and *Psychocybernetics* by Maxwell Maltz can be very helpful. There are a number of such books in the library and available as paperbacks in bookstores. The books have one fault; that is, they lead one to believe that if he only has a positive attitude, everything will turn out all right. This is a little too simple. It often takes more than positive thinking. It may take the right circumstances, the right behavior, ability, help from others, and so

on. However, all things being equal, it will go better if we think
positively. Such thinking helps us make the best of most situations
and facilitates success, even if it is not enough in itself to assure that
success. Books on positive thinking often contain helpful hints on
good ways to assert one's self and provide support and encouragement to go ahead and try. They are well worth reading if we keep
them in perspective.

chapter nine

PROBLEM SOLVING,

DECISION MAKING,

AND BRAINSTORMING

Often acute anxiety develops when we are faced with solving some problem or making a decision. This can be true of any type of decision, but it is especially true if the decision is a very important one. We find ourselves struggling with the problem of deciding. One minute we feel one way, the next minute we feel the other way. We worry that maybe we will make the wrong decision. We wish there were some way to determine the right thing to do. The more we put off making the decision, the more anxious we get. We know that we must make a decision, but we don't know what to do. The tension becomes excruciating. We can't sleep. We lose our appetite and become preoccupied with the decision we have to make. Some people have this kind of difficulty with little decisions as well as big ones. Other people have problems making decisions in some areas but not in others. In this chapter we will present some of the ways to make good decisions.

One simple way is to sit down and try to make the process more concrete. Often we have a number of vague ideas, fears, concerns, etc., in our heads, but since we have not really put them into words, they are very hard to handle. A good procedure is to sit down with a piece of paper. Draw a line down the middle and put the reasons for a certain course of action on one side and the reasons against it on the other. Study the lists and try to weigh your feelings. Often putting the reasons into words clarifies our thinking. Then, seeing them on paper in front of us helps us weigh the alternatives and make a decision. Sometimes it helps to make the list and put it away for awhile. Later when you come back, the decision may be very easy. Or you may add or subtract from the list and then make the decision. At any rate, this technique does help clarify your thinking and move you toward actually making the decision instead of thinking about it in a very vague, disorganized manner.

A technique for problem solving and decision making that was pioneered by Alex Osborn is called "brainstorming." The process of brainstorming is very simple and very effective. Brainstorming is basically a procedure for groups, but it can be used as an individual technique also. To use it in groups, get some people together who are interested and cooperative. Somewhere around five to ten seems to work best, but often two or three are adequate. Specify as clearly as possible exactly what problem the session is to focus on. Then start generating ideas according to the four basic rules for brainstorming:

1. **Critical judgment of ideas is ruled out.** Criticism and evaluation of ideas will come later. Criticism of your own ideas or of the ideas of other people is stifling and inhibiting of creativity. It is not permitted during the session.

2. **"Free-wheeling" is encouraged.** Try to come up with wild, unusual ideas. Ideas that are new and different are wanted. After all, if more conventional or obvious ideas contained easy solutions, we would not be so stumped by the problem. It is often easy to take a wild idea and tame it, making it a very creative and valuable solution to a problem.

3. **Quantity is what is wanted.** What is desired in the session is quantity, not quality. The goal is to come up with as many ideas as possible. Research has shown that a larger number of *good* ideas actually are developed when we express all ideas that come to us than when we evaluate them and express only the "good" ideas.

4. **Combination and improvement are sought.** As ideas are expressed, each person should think of ways to extend them,

revise them, or combine them with other ideas to produce still other ideas or combinations. In generating and revising ideas, consider such points as: what other uses could this object or idea be put to in its present form (uses that have not been thought of or tried before)? What uses would be possible if this object or idea were adapted or modified in some way? What would happen if we maximized or minimized one aspect or effect? What if we changed the order and did it in a different sequence?

There is good evidence that using brainstorming techniques produces excellent results. Some of the ways it seems to work are that one person's thoughts and ideas often stir up another person's associations, stimulating him to come up with ideas and thoughts that he would not have on his own, and vice versa. Also, the social motivation and facilitation of being in a group of people working on a problem enables us to work more diligently and enthusiastically than we would on our own. In addition, the stimulating effects of competition and friendly rivalry contribute to greater productivity.

There is the old story about the community stew. One person had carrots, another a potato, another a piece of meat, and so on. When they stayed home, they all ate a meager and unbalanced diet. But, when they got together and put what they had in a pot in the center of town, there was enough for everyone to feast healthily.

If you want to use group brainstorming to work on a problem, get a group of people together who are as motivated and concerned about the problem as you are. They might be friends who have interests similar to yours. If the problem is job related, they might be people you work with or who are in a similar line of work. They might be family members if it is a family problem. Incidentally, don't hesitate to include children in such sessions. Often they come up with some of the really outstandingly fresh and creative approaches. It is interesting to brainstorm such things as income tax deductions, ways to save money around the house, how to get a job at work done more quickly and easily.

While two heads are better than one, and groups do better at brainstorming than individuals, this does not mean that you cannot do it alone. You can. Just sit quietly and let ideas flow, following the same rules as above. You can do it at home, in your office, while traveling somewhere, or anytime. The main value of brainstorming is to generate ideas. One thing that often hinders decision making is inhibition of ideas. This is often because the person has developed what psychologists call rigidity in his thinking. To be rigid in your thinking means that you can only see one or two ways of approaching a problem and are not able to look at it from different points of view. If one of the solutions you are able to see works, then everything is O.K.; if not, you are in trouble. Such rigid thinking often leads to anxiety over problems that can be solved easily if we can break out of the rigid mold in which we find ourselves.

As ideas are generated during brainstorming, it is best to simply write them down as they come. Later go over them and evaluate them. Following this, prepare a new list containing some of the better ones. After some study and thought, prepare a list with what you consider to be the best alternative at the top and the least desirable one at the bottom. That way, you can try the first one and see if it works. If it does, you have solved the problem. If not, go to the next alternative and continue in this manner until you find one that works.

Ordering the alternatives in terms of their desirability requires that you consider several features of each alternative. This is, of course, the hardest part of the task. You may remember the old story about the farmhand who worked very diligently for his boss. When he was in the fields, nobody could keep up with him; he could do twice as much as other men. In addition, he seemed to enjoy and thrive on hard work. One day when it was particularly hot, the boss decided to give the man a break. He went and got him from the fields and took him into the barn where it was cool and where he could sit down instead of working so hard. His job was to sort the potatoes according to size into three piles—small, medium, and large. At the end of the day, the boss came back and was shocked to see that his best worker had hardly sorted any potatoes at all! Puzzled, he asked him what the problem was. The man replied, "It's these damned decisions."

One of the first things to consider in ordering the possible alternatives is their irreversibility. There are some that you can try and if they don't work, no particular harm will have been done. You can simply go on to another one. However, some of the alternatives, once tried, make further solutions harder to accomplish. Such alternatives should generally be placed farther down on the list.

A second consideration is the amount of effort required for trying one of the solutions. If it is easy to do, it may be worth trying and should tend to be placed closer to the top of the list than one that is very difficult or that takes a lot of time and effort.

A third consideration is the risk involved. If an alternative is attempted, what are the risks? What are things that might go wrong and what would be the consequences if they did? Obviously, risky ones will tend to be lower on the list.

Another consideration is the probability that the alternative will work. Some are long shots and others are almost sure things. This needs to be taken into account.

Finally, keeping the above principles in mind, we must consider the ultimate payoff. If we try a given solution and it works, how will it benefit us?

Using these principles, we will find that they are combined in various mixtures in the possible alternatives. With some thought, we can order them according to our preference and start to try them. I often like to start with a long shot which doesn't take too much effort, will not be at all irreversible, and which would have a large payoff—if such an alternative exists. If you don't have a dream, it can't come true. But if you try for your dream, sometimes you will obtain it. If it doesn't work, however, I then proceed down the list. The solutions I put on the bottom are ones that require a lot of effort, are irreversible, are pretty sure of working, but tend to have minimal payoff. Different people may prefer different strategies, and we may have different strategies in different situations. The important thing is to have a strategy and to execute it.

Some people find it helpful to write out their list of alternatives and check them off as they are tried. Others just keep them in mind. Putting them down on paper often makes one feel better and facilitates clear thinking and action.

There are some additional principles of decision making that are well to keep in mind. One is that in the majority of the situations we face, *only we can really make the decision.* Relying on somebody else to tell us what to do will generally not lead to satisfactory results. As is often said, advice is easy to give but hard to take. If a group of people happen to be involved, we may want to make the decision by committee vote, but the majority of decisions that we face and that produce anxiety are matters only we can decide. We may as well face up to this and do so assertively.

Secondly, we need to realize that the process of decision making is one in which we will sometimes make what might be considered the wrong decision. Actually, if we follow the principles outlined in this chapter, it will not be wrong. We will have made the best decision possible under the circumstances. Sometimes, however, the outcome may not be what we wanted it to be. When that happens, we need to philosophically accept the fact that everybody wins some and loses some—ourselves included. The main point is to learn from each experience so that we can win more than we lose.

Third, it helps a great deal if we practice reinforcing ourselves after we have made a decision. To do this, we can say something to ourselves like, "Well, I made the best decision possible as the situation presented itself. That's all I could do. I did what I thought was right and that's what a person ought to do. I'm glad I did it. I fulfilled my responsibility." Later, if someone else has a different idea or if things don't turn out the way you wanted, you can be open to learning from the situation. You need not feel defensive or upset because you have already settled it within yourself that you honestly and sincerely did what you considered to be the right thing and you feel good about that part. If a revision is called for, you are free to go ahead with that as part two of the process. You will then also reinforce yourself for doing that. The point is that you are monitoring your own behavior and doing what you think is right. This makes you a person of integrity and self-confidence. You are receptive to feedback from others, but you make up your own mind.

It is this balance that makes a mature, responsible person. If we are overly stubborn about our own ideas, we are not fair to others. If we are overly dependent on what others *think* we ought to do in a situation, we are wishy-washy and lack personal integrity. This makes us anxious and miserable. Successful decision making takes a balance of responsiveness to feedback and internal judgment. The fulcrum is self-reinforcement.

chapter ten

NUTRITION AND EXERCISE

When I was a boy going to school in Madison, Ohio, we used to have a grade school teacher named "Pop" Ryan. He was about 70 years old but was in excellent health and full of vigor. He was a man of the old school and used to lecture us on the importance of maintaining good health and hygiene practices. It was the old "sound mind in a healthy body" theory. We used to snicker at him while eating excessive quantities of hamburgers and french fries, with a soft drink to wash them down. We knew our diet would have caused his hair to stand on end, but we regarded him as sort of a "kook." It's funny, though, over the years as I learned more and more about physical and mental health, I began to discover that the old guy had something. I've found in terms of my own experience and in clinical work with my patients that physical and mental health often go together. When we are tense, anxious, and depressed, we feel physical pain and general malaise. Also, when we are physically ill, for example, when we come down with a cold or the flu, we often feel emotionally upset, depressed, and anxious. Good physical health contributes to good mental health and vice versa.

Consider general nutrition. Food has special significance for many people. Since we are often comforted with food as children, we tend to associate food with love and security. Thus, many people find that they eat when they are anxious or tense. Eating makes them feel better, temporarily. It is interesting to note that certain kinds of food or food prepared in certain ways may have the same effect. For example, many people find that very spicy foods, such as Italian or Mexican dishes, tend to cause discomfort. This may be the effect of such foods on some people. However, I was reared on food prepared by a wonderful Italian mother. As a result, eating spicy foods actually has a calming and settling effect on my stomach. Some of my physiologically oriented friends tell me that isn't possible, but that's the way it works for me.

Various claims are made from time to time that, beyond their contribution to good nutrition, eating certain foods, organically grown foods, uncooked food, or some special diet, such as a strictly vegetarian diet, will result in better physical health and possibly improve mental health. There is no scientific evidence to support these claims at present. However, many of these claims have not been thoroughly studied. Perhaps eventually we will find that there is some truth to them. At present, trained nutritionists are cautious about making any claims for such eating habits until there is sound scientific support for them. It is well known that nutritional deficiencies result in declining health and disease, which are often accompanied by mental and emotional symptoms of one sort or another. Therefore, a well-balanced diet certainly contributes to the general energy level, stamina, and sense of well-being in an individual.

Some rules for good nutrition that are generally endorsed by physicians and nutritionists are to avoid overeating and overweight. Eat several smaller meals each day rather than large meals. Eat a balanced diet each day. A balanced diet is one which includes the four basic food groups of (1) milk, cheese, and other dairy products, (2) meat, (3) vegetables and fruit, and (4) bread and cereals. It is also well to avoid too many fried foods and excessive consumption of sweets.

It is a good practice to eat slowly, chewing food carefully. You should also make mealtime a time of relaxing. Rather than eating hurriedly, gulping your food, and conducting business during meals, try taking a walk, reading, resting, listening to music, or some such activity to unwind a little *before the meal.* Then, sit down and enjoy a leisurely, relaxed meal. You'll enjoy the food much more, take the edge off daily anxiety, and reduce the likelihood of developing ulcers.

There is currently some debate about nutrition in the United States. Some say our food storage and preparation methods reduce the nutritional value of the food we consume. Others insist that we are the healthiest and best fed people who have ever lived. Still others say that while perfectly adequate foods are available to Americans, their eating habits do not provide them with the proper selection to produce a balanced diet. Nutritionists recommend following a balanced diet (which includes foods from each of the basic groups) as the best remedy. That will be quite sufficient for most people's good health. No further supplement such as "health foods" or vitamins should be needed. There is a lot of faddism in this area. Physicians are quick to point out that fad diets, large doses of vitamins, and similar practices may be dangerous and harmful to some people. Therefore, if you feel you are one of the exceptions that requires some dietary supplement, consult a physician who is trained in nutrition. Many physicians are not familiar with this area, but your family physician can help you locate one who is. He can examine you and prescribe the right supplement or medication for you, if you need it. Doing this will enable you to get exactly what you need in a safe, supervised manner. Experimenting on your own can be dangerous.

Exercise is also very effective in reducing anxiety. How this occurs is not entirely understood. Some say that it satisfies the evolutionary need of man to engage in large muscle, physically aggressive activity that was adaptive in primitive man but which with our highly civilized, sedentary, and confined life style has no other outlet.

Physiologically, exercise affects all the systems of the body. Circulation of blood and consumption of oxygen are increased. Body temperature rises. Metabolism is stepped up. Waste products are excreted more rapidly from the cells and are eventually eliminated from the body through perspiration, urination, and defecation.

Prolonged exercise tends to produce an oxygen deficit and an increased level of lactic acid in the blood. Paradoxically, these are usually associated with the occurrence of anxiety, rather than its reduction, but in the case of exercise, it does seem to reduce anxiety and tension, making one feel better.

Over a period of time, vital capacity is increased by exercise. Circulation and oxygen utilization is improved and a larger exertion is required before lactic acid is produced. It is possible that this serves as a sort of anxiety-inhibiting mechanism.

Whatever the basis for it, exercise does have an anxiety- and tension-reducing effect. Studies have shown that people on regular exercise programs tend to be more healthy, have better vital capacity, handle problems better, sleep better, and cope with life in a generally more satisfactory manner. Over a period of time, people on such programs generally feel better, are more optimistic, and have a better self-image. Thus, exercise immediately reduces anxiety somewhat and over the long run it tends to inoculate us against development of future anxieties.

Exercise, however, can be very dangerous if too strenuous or of the wrong type for a person's physical condition. In general, the older one is, the more cautious he needs to be, but youth is no guarantee that harm will not occur. Every year young people engaged in athletic activities suffer heart attacks, strokes, and other complications. Before beginning an exercise program, it is very important to consult your family physician for advice.

There are two basic types of exercise that can be employed to reduce anxiety. One is rhythmic motion. Such activities as walking, running, swimming, bicycling provide rhythmic motion. Jogging has become a very popular exercise of this type. The aerobics programs of Dr. Kenneth Cooper are very fine. As Dr. Cooper points out, such exercise not only reduces anxiety, it also increases general health, aids in weight reduction, and helps to prevent heart disease and various other disorders. His books are available in paperback form at all bookstores.

The other major type of exercise is stretching. You may have noticed that people frequently stretch their arms above their head in times of tension to help relieve the discomfort. This basic technique can be used much more extensively. For example, if you feel tension in the neck, take your head in your hands and gently stretch it. Then hold the head and chin and exert pressure downward, again stretching the neck muscles. If the back is tense, bend and stretch in ways that pull the muscles gently. If your chest is tight, make some stretching movements in various directions with the arms until the tension and tightness subsides. Practicing exercises of this sort on a regular basis can be very beneficial.

When I encourage patients to exercise for anxiety reduction, I generally point out to them that to do the most good, the exercise should be a regular activity. Therefore, it should be worked into their life style somehow. Many people exercise first thing in the morning. They then take a shower and go to work. I had a friend who was a university professor. He used to jog from his home to the university. He had a locker in the gym where he showered and dressed for classes after he arrived. Some people exercise when they get home from work or just before bedtime. Most cities of any size have groups who get together during their lunch hour at the Y or at one of the commercial health centers. Some companies provide facilities for exercise. But whenever or wherever one does it, *regular* exercise is the key.

If you have other physical problems, exercise can be recommended by your physician or by a physical therapist to help with them as a secondary benefit. For example, I have a shoulder that pops out of place easily and a back that was injured while I was in high school. Both tend to give me a lot of pain from time to time. I consulted a physical therapist and learned some exercises to incorporate into my own routine exercise program. When I do these exercises regularly, my shoulder stays in place and my back gives me no trouble. As my fellow sufferers know, these are no small benefits.

Since many people can't get too excited about getting up an hour earlier to jog or giving up their lunch hour to do so, I recommend that they choose a sport they like and play it regularly for the exercise. Tennis, handball, golf, boating, swimming, and many others are good for this.

Be sure to consult a physician before you begin an exercise

program. Then, start out gradually and build up rather than trying to do too much too soon.

Many people find hot baths to be very relaxing. These can be taken on their own or following exercise. Simply fill the tub with hot water (about as hot as you can stand it) and lie in it until the muscles relax. You should be careful not to relax too much because it is possible to fall asleep, and drowning is a risk. Even more effective are whirlpool baths. Small units can be purchased for home bathtubs. Most exercise centers have them available. The whirlpool turbines circulate the water adding a gentle massage action to the benefits of the heat from the water. Hot baths seem to have their effect in several ways. Circulation is increased, metabolic activity of the cells is accelerated, waste products are carried away more rapidly, and the muscle tissue relaxes. It is a purgative process. While the reason is not fully understood, pain is also reduced under these circumstances. Soreness and stiffness following exercise is less likely to occur if a hot bath is taken immediately after.

Some people find alternating heat and cold to be very effective. This can be harmful for some, however, especially if they have any type of circulatory problem. Therefore, it is best to check with your physician on this before you try it. After checking, if you decide to try this, first take a hot bath or shower and stay under the hot water for four or five minutes. Then turn the hot water off and turn cold water on for about two minutes.

Actually heat appears to have many of these effects regardless of how it is applied. The benefits of sauna and steam baths are derived in essentially the same manner. If you plan to use sauna or steam baths, it is important to familiarize yourself with the equipment and use it properly. Talk to someone familiar with the equipment you are using and read the manufacturer's manual. In general, the rules for safe use of sauna and steam baths are as follows:

First, sauna and steam baths can be dangerous for some people—the elderly, people suffering from diabetes, heart disease, high blood pressure, as well as numerous other conditions. In addition, there are dangers if you have ingested alcohol, antihistamines, anticoagulants, narcotics, tranquilizers, sedatives, or other medications. Therefore, as with the other activities suggested in this chapter, you should consult your physician before you begin. A phone call to your family physician will suffice. If you do not have a family physician, use this as a good opportunity to get a physical exam and discuss your plans with the physician who examines you.

Second, be sure to read and follow the directions of the manufacturer of the equipment or of the person supervising the equipment. Do not use the equipment alone. Someone should be around to help if necessary. There should be a window for them to check on you and there should be a clock clearly visible so you will know how long you have been in. If you are a beginner, start out with just a couple of minutes, no more than five. Gradually increase to a level that feels good. Never stay in more than a maximum of twenty to thirty minutes.

Do not exercise strenuously before sauna or steam baths and do not exercise at all while in them. Do not enter them for at least an hour after eating a full meal. Drink liquids before and after.

Proper use of sauna and steam baths will reduce weight (though it is only water loss and will return shortly), increase circulation, lead to muscular relaxation, and possibly improve and clear the skin. There is no evidence that they prevent or cure the common cold. They are not recommended for people whose sinuses are draining or as a cure for hangover.

Massage can have a similarly relaxing and beneficial effect. Massage increases circulation and metabolism in the same way heat does. However, it appears to offer additional advantages. The mechanics of massage force fluid out of the tissues, thus improving circulation and reducing swelling and pressure due to excessive fluid that sometimes gathers, especially following trauma or exercise. Also, the mechanical stretching of the muscles and connective tissues tends to relax them and reduce pain. Massage must be done properly to be of much help. Most health centers, many Y's, and similar clubs have trained masseurs available. Physical therapists also, of course, provide massage. Generally, a referral from a physician is required before a physical therapist can see you, but this is not hard to obtain. In smaller towns, interested people sometimes arrange with a nurse, physical education teacher, or a trainer for the school athletes to provide massage. Many find that a good massage reduces anxiety remarkably and makes a new person out of them.

My experience has been that it takes a lot of encouragement to get people to try the things mentioned in this chapter, but when they do, they invariably report that the techniques work and that they never felt better in their lives. These techniques appear to reduce anxiety as well as improve the general health and stamina of the person. A regular program can involve minutes or hours per day, but it appears to be time well spent.

chapter eleven

RECREATION AND ESCAPE

Anxious people don't have much fun in life. When we are anxious, we suffer such mental anguish and physical pain that we cannot enjoy ourselves. It is also true that if we live a life without much provision for having fun, we become more susceptible to anxiety. Thus it tends to work both ways and, eventually, we get into a terrible rut. We are anxious so much of the time that we can't enjoy ourselves, and not enjoying ourselves tends to make us more anxious and depressed.

There are a number of factors that seem to push us in this direction. Often it starts with very real tensions and problems that, if left unresolved, eventually get us down. Then we get into the anxiety rut. Paradoxically, sometimes we become so familiar with our anxiety rut that we are afraid to venture out of it. We wallow in it and never venture out because at least we know it, and know it well. Other alternatives seem vague, unfamiliar, and possibly even more threatening. Sam Keen puts it almost poetically. In his book *To a Dancing God* (New York: Harper & Row, 1970, pp. 109–110), he records a dialogue he had with fear. Part of it goes like this:

SAM KEEN: I wish I could begin by saying, "Damn you fear. Leave me alone!" But honesty demands that I address you as "Dear fear," for you have been with me most of my life. Now I want to understand why I am attracted to you and did not banish you long ago.

FEAR: I am glad you are willing to admit that we are reluctant friends. It has taken me some years to get you to confess that you are a hesitant lover of what you pretend to despise. What a capacity for self-deceit you have, pretending that I was somehow your fated enemy! Or, to be specific, that I was an unconscious legacy from your parents. Such transparent nonsense. If I am your fate, I am at least a fate you have chosen and nurtured. It is not without your consent and satisfaction that we have been together all these years. You might have lived in conversation with love, or courage, or creativity, or desire, or fame. No! You have kept me around. So don't try to disown me.

Sometimes we get into an anxiety rut by failing to play. Our society teaches us that work is good and, for adults, play is evil. It is a sinful waste of time and talent. As we become adults, we are supposed to grow out of our need for it. If we don't, we are stupid and immature. The ultimate believer in this has been called a "workoholic." A workoholic is a person who is not happy if he is not working at something. He can't get enough of it to satisfy him. He may work long hours at one, two, or more jobs. When he goes home, he takes work with him and thinks of things to do around the house. Idle time makes him nervous. Weekends are an agony and vacations drag because he can't wait to get back to work. Housewives often show the same pattern, in working from early morning until late at night seven days a week. Their houses and families are excessively attended to. No time is left for resting. Workoholics have a lot of the same problems as alcoholics. Their obsession with work destroys their family and interpersonal lives, ruins their health (heart attacks, ulcers, etc.), and eventually leaves them desolate. In many cases, such a person would actually have been more productive *in the long run* if he didn't overdo working early in his life.

As people have often pointed out, the word *recreation* may be thought of as re-creation. The respite and escape we derive from play, refreshes us and makes us able to go back and do more later. It enables us to continue to be more productive longer.

It is interesting that a very common symptom of emotional disturbance is withdrawal. The person who is emotionally disturbed often isolates himself from friends, reneges on responsibilities, and turns off to life. He becomes unresponsive, uncommunicative, and unproductive. What has happened at this point is that his problems have overwhelmed him, and he is unable to handle them. Thus he retreats from them and gives up completely. As is the case with many of the symptoms of emotional disturbance, this massive retreat from life is just an exaggeration of a more normal response that everyone makes. We all need to get away from our problems and responsibilities from time to time. Play and recreation can be a "tactical retreat," enabling us to come back better and stronger later. If we use it that way, massive retreat into emotional disturbance will not be necessary. Thus, in order to live a productive life and keep anxiety at a minimum, we need to have adequate recreation and escape.

There are many ways we can do this. First, we need to relearn the way to play. If we have been anxious for a long time or are veteran workoholics, we may have to reach back into the past and search our memories to find things we can do for play. If we really think about it, we can come up with some. It is important that we begin to do things we like to do and that give us pleasure. Often they are things we have always wanted to do but couldn't seem to find time for.

Some people enjoy walks or hikes. Others like to play a sport such as tennis or golf. Some people like to go on picnics, while others would rather try out a new restaurant. Some people go to plays or movies for escape. Others prefer athletic events. Some take one- or two-day trips out of town, others prefer to stay home and play a game or watch T.V. Many people like to shop or browse. Some like to cook. Others like to listen to music or play an instrument. There are hundreds of things people do for recreation. You should do some of the ones you like. If it has been so long since you did them that you really don't feel like it, *force yourself.* You have to start somewhere.

When you engage in these activities, practice clearing your mind of all that has been preoccupying you. Then, become totally absorbed in the activity you have chosen. It takes a little effort and practice to be able to do that, but you can train yourself to do so. Thought stopping, mentioned in chapter seven, is often helpful in keeping your mind clear of thoughts that would prevent you from enjoying play.

Once you learn to put worries out of your mind and become absorbed in play, you will find that these activities provide great satisfaction and enjoyment. They will add a new dimension of richness to your life. You will begin to see them as islands of refuge and refreshment. If you do them frequently, they become a major source of pleasure. You will be continuously thinking of the fun of the last experience and looking forward to the next. This makes life more exciting and enables us to do a better job at the more difficult tasks we face.

Developing a hobby can serve much the same purpose. Many people find satisfaction, reward, fulfillment, and escape in a hobby. A survey done at the Menninger Clinic some years ago indicated that there was a positive relationship between being significantly involved in a hobby and good mental health.

It is also a good idea to participate in a wide variety of recreational activities. When children learn to play, they play alone at first. Later, they develop parallel play; that is, they play at things alone, but side by side. For example, they may each be swinging, playing with toy cars, or building sand castles, but they are not interacting with each other as part of the play. Still later, children begin to play together. They cooperate and interact in their play. As adults, we can use all of these of types of play. We may want to have a hobby or some form of recreation that we do alone. In addition, we may want to read or paint or pursue some similar activity while family members or friends do something parallel. At other times, we will want to interact and cooperate as in playing cards, chess, etc. This satisfies our need for a variety of experiences in life. As we begin to have more fun, we will find that we are more relaxed and less anxious. Periodic escape from everyday problems refreshes us and allows us to see the problems of living in perspective.

Many people are so indoctrinated in the work ethic that they are not able to play or relax until they have first finished all their work. Of course, this is a trap because we never finish all our work. Consequently, we never have occasion to play. A good way to handle this is to develop work-play contingencies. To do this, you need to specify a given task or portion of a task that needs to be done. You then say to yourself, "When I finish that I will be entitled to a few hours of play for recreation and refreshment." You can then do the job and go play golf, go to a movie, or whatever you wish. Making play contingent on completing the work is good for a couple of reasons. First, it motivates you to get the work done quicker and you are happier while you are doing it because you know that you are getting closer and closer to your recreation time. Second, you can enjoy the play without feeling guilty because it is a reward for having done a significant job, which is now completed. Putting work and play in this type of juxtaposition makes for a productive and happy life style.

Of course, you should also practice self-reinforcement at these times. Say to yourself, "That's good. I got that job done. I'm glad I did it. Now I'm going to go play golf. I'll get to that other job first thing tomorrow when I'm fresh and relaxed. It will go better then."

One other problem is that some people set their goals too high. They pick a job that is too big to accomplish with enough time left over for play. The result, of course, is that they never quite get around to playing. If that is your problem, schedule a certain number of play hours after a specified number of hours of work rather than after completion of the job. You can say, "I'm going to work on the yard for four hours in the morning on Saturday. Then, I'm going to relax and watch the ball game on TV. What I don't get done in that four hours, I'll do next Saturday. But, I'm really going to work hard during those four hours." If you do this, you will find that Parkinson's Law often applies to this type of situation. One of Parkinson's laws states that work will expand or contract to fit the time provided to do it in. If you have three or four things to do in the yard and have set no time limit, they may take all day. However, if you set a four-hour time limit, you will generally get all or most all of them done in that amount of time, if you really try. Then, you will have four hours for relaxation, and you've still accomplished the same amount in terms of work.

One final word. If you are determined to have fun in life, often you can even approach work playfully and enjoy it more than you otherwise might. Suppose you have a rather boring task to do—perhaps peeling apples for a pie. If there are two people working at it, they can each take an equal number of apples and race to see who finishes first. The loser has to peel the remaining apples or clean up the mess afterwards. This is, of course, a very simple example, but the point is that if you make an effort and use a little creativity, a lot of things in life can be approached playfully and enjoyed rather than endured. Such an approach to work and play is an antidote to much of the anxiety we experience daily.

chapter twelve

FRIENDS AND COMMUNICATION

Human beings find considerable support and comfort in close relationships with others. The poet John Donne put it so well that his words have been quoted over and over:

> No man is an island, entire of itself; every man is a piece of the Continent, a part of the main; if a clod be washed away by the sea, Europe is the less, as well as if a manor of thy friends or of thine own were; any man's death diminishes me, because I am involved in mankind; and therefore never send to know for whom the bell tolls; it tolls for thee.

Having friends and being able to communicate meaningfully with them is a great bulwark against anxiety. It used to be that the immediate family and the extended family (aunts, uncles, grandparents, cousins, etc.) gave stability to people's lives and offered support in times of crisis. The extended family gave the individual a context in which to view himself. There were frequent family gatherings, with stories about the history of the family in terms of what various relatives had done and were doing. There was a security in knowing that one was not alone. There were people who cared and who could be called upon for help in times of crisis such as births, deaths, illnesses, and financial problems. There were no questions asked. It was family. People did what had to be done to see each other through.

However, more recently, with the increased mobility of people, the increasing tempo of our lives, and the development of generation gaps, the family often is no longer able to fulfill such needs. Generally, the members are scattered all over the country. They are busy with their own lives, and distance prevents them from developing a feeling of being closely tied to the others. The expense and disruption of living required for them to come to the aid of a cousin or brother often seem too great a sacrifice. Many young people purposely arrange their lives in this manner. They want to be away from their families and on their own. As someone has said, fate provides us with family; fortunately, we can choose our friends. However, facing crises under such circumstances can be very stressful and anxiety provoking.

For many people, friends take the place of the extended family. There are, of course, different levels of friendship. We all have a fairly large number of friends who are people we know in the sense that we recognize each other and carry on conversation when we happen to meet. There are other friends whom we enjoy being around sufficiently that we seek out occasions when we can meet. There are still other friends that we feel very close to. People with whom we share important aspects of our lives and whom we can call on anytime we are in need. It is a good idea to have friends of all these types. They all add a dimension to our lives in their own unique way.

Unfortunately many people have trouble making friends. There are, however, some rules that help in making and keeping friends. First, as is often pointed out, the best way to have friends is to be a friend. That's an interesting and succinct way of putting it, but it is important to understand what it means. It means that if we want to have friends, we need to do the things that make friends of people. When we meet people, we need to come out of our shell and become interested in *them* and their world. Often we are so preoccupied with our world and so concerned about whether or not we will make a good impression that we never really make contact with an individual we have just met. It is important to forget ourselves and reach out to others when we meet them. Try to tune in on who they are and what they are interested in. Remember, a stranger is just a friend you haven't met yet. Once we find out a little about a person, we can share some of our thoughts and experiences with him. It also helps to smile a little and express pleasure about something he mentions.

A second rule is that in order to develop friendships, we must develop a great deal of acceptance and patience. We must accept people as they are and not expect them to try to change to suit us. Fritz Perls put it very well in his prayer when he said of others that they were not here to measure up to his expectations, nor he to theirs. He goes on to say that we are to do our own thing and be ourselves. If we develop a relationship in the process, that is wonderful; if not, it cannot be helped.

Of course, as a person gets to know and associate with us, he may change, but that must not be one of the conditions of friendship. Good friendship develops out of a certain amount of unconditional positive regard. People often do what we don't like and we could take offense at this. But it is necessary to overlook a lot of these things and forget them. We have to realize that people are "just that way." They are not perfect. They also will have to overlook our shortcomings. We have to realize that people have faults and decide to be their friend anyway.

As a friendship develops, you can strengthen and enhance it by doing small favors and showing little kindnesses to the person. Being able to graciously accept similar favors from others is the other side of the coin. Some people are quite willing to do things for others, but cannot bring themselves to let anyone do something for them. It is important to develop the ability to give and to receive.

Given the above rules for making friends, there are two further points to keep in mind. One is that to make friends we have to come in contact with people who are potential friends. We can't sit at home and expect them to come and find us. There are numerous ways to come in contact with potential friends. We can invite people to our home for dinner, parties, or get-togethers. We can go to places where we will meet people: churches are good places, as are civic clubs, hobby groups, and discussion groups. If we get involved in community and social activities, we will make friends of some of the people we come in contact with.

The second point is that it is seldom possible to force friendship on someone. Friendship is a lot like a love relationship in this sense. Some people will like us and a friendship will develop. Others, for a variety of reasons, will not, and a friendship will not develop. Real friendship has to be something that "clicks" between people. It cannot be forced and doesn't work if it is one-sided. We need to spend our time and energy selecting and developing friends from those who are interested rather than lamenting the fact that some people we would like to be friendly with do not seem interested.

Psychologists frequently refer to friendship as being based on patterns of mutual reinforcement. Essentially, what this means is that if the way a person looks, acts, thinks, and feels is pleasing to us, we will want to spend more time in that person's company. We say that being with this individual is fun. It is reinforcing and rewarding to us. If he or she feels the same way about us, a friendship develops. This principle explains a lot of things about friendship. For example, our friendships change over the years. We may no longer enjoy being with people we once liked. People we once had little time for may come to be our best and closest friends. If we analyze what has happened, we often find that our needs and style of living have changed over the years so that the people whose behavior is rewarding to us have changed. Likewise, it is often said that the best friends are made by a common enemy. In this case, both are rewarded by working toward goals that defeat the third party. Such people are often close friends until the third party departs the scene for some reason, then they drift apart and wonder how they ever could have been friends. The source of mutual reinforcement has been removed.

One of the best features of having friends is communication. Man is the only animal that communicates by means of a complex language and symbol system. Hours spent in conversation with close friends are stimulating, rewarding, and anxiety reducing. Often just getting something off our chest by telling a friend about it makes us feel much better. Frequently, friends are able to extend support or share some of their experiences with us. This can make a difference. Many times just getting our thoughts into words clarifies our thinking and cuts through the nebulous quality of what is troubling us. When we clarify our thoughts and feelings, often they are seen to be not really so frightening. They seemed worse than they really were mainly because we had not pinned them down and looked at them objectively.

Good communication between friends demands trust between the two. We need to feel free to tell them what we want to say. We need to be able to trust them in handling the information we give. Some people will be ruled out of this depth of friendship, but those we include will be people of special importance. Actually, a tragedy of many people's lives is that they often overlook the fact that a husband or wife can be their best friend. He or she is, after all, a person who cares and who is deeply involved with you for better or for worse. We need to communicate with and cultivate them as one of our best friends. Strange to say, most marriage relationships unfortunately exist on a more superficial and defensive level than this.

While we need to have trust in our friends, they need to have empathy for us. Empathy is the ability to understand and fully appreciate how a person feels while still remaining objective about it. It is different from sympathy. In sympathy you feel the same emotion as the person and become involved in the same experience as he. This reduces your ability to be objective and to effectively help him. For example, if someone is grieving and you sympathize with the person, you begin to feel bad and grieve also. At that point you both feel bad and you are not able to help much. However, if you were feeling empathy, you would fully appreciate how the person really felt but maintain enough objectivity to accurately perceive the situation. You would then be able to see workable solutions and go about putting them into operation. The result of empathy is help.

Communication involves two processes: talking and listening. People may have trouble with either or both. Some people have trouble talking. They find it difficult to put their ideas and feelings into words. Many times they don't know the right words to use. Other times they know the words but are afraid to say them for fear they will get an unfavorable response. If you have trouble talking, you need first to find a friend you trust and who has the ability to empathize with you. Then, you need to force yourself to talk to that person about your thoughts and feelings. You may start out with little things and short conversations if you wish and build up to more important and more extensive conversations later. But you *must* begin to talk. Not even friends can read your mind.

Some people who find it difficult to talk write letters and notes to others when an occasion arises. Often, they can express their deeper feelings much more accurately this way. It is easy to do this by writing a note on a birthday, Christmas, or anniversary card. There are also cards designed just to say thanks or to send a brief thought to a person. In addition, you can write to others when you are out of town or they are, during vacations, for example. A friend used to write notes to her husband and put them in with his lunch. He really looked forward to reading her notes while he ate. It gave both him and her a great lift each day.

The other side of communication is listening. We need to learn to listen to what people say to us. Sometimes this means just being quiet long enough for them to say what they want to. Often we have a tendency to interrupt or to jump to conclusions before the other person has finished talking. It is an art worth developing to be able to hear a person out and let them say, in their own words, what they want to say. Of course, you also need to be sure that you really understand what they mean. You need to take in and carefully analyze what they are saying. You need to shake loose from your own conceptual framework and see things within their framework and their value system before you can really understand. It does no good to apply your own value system to the situation and discard as unimportant, facts or details that the other person considers very important.

A useful technique when you are not sure just how a person thinks or feels about an area is to say something like, "I'm not sure I follow, but what you seem to be saying is this. . . ." Then repeat the sense of what the other person said, as best you can interpret it. The other can either agree with or correct your statement.

It is, of course, also important to sometimes go behind the words the person is saying and tune in to the real underlying feelings. The tone of voice, physical posture, and gestures may all reveal anxiety, frustration, anger, joy, and other emotions that are not obvious from the words being used in the conversation. Generally, if you pay attention to these cues you will communicate and understand much better. If you are pretty sure of the message coming from these cues, you can respond to the content of the words and the subtle cues without necessarily labeling them and making a major point of letting the person know you have picked them up. This often results in a feeling of warmth and friendship that says, "You understand me. I know you do. Thanks." Of course, you have to be sure you have correctly interpreted these cues, or you may eventually run into a blank wall or lose contact with the person. If you seem to be headed in that direction, it is often helpful to stop and say something like, "I'm not sure I fully understand. Do you seem to feel this way?" You can then label the feeling you think you picked up from the cues. The other, again, can agree with or correct your impression.

Relationships based on positive regard, patience, trust, and empathy are true and lasting friendships that comfort us in times of crisis and serve as bulwarks against many of the stresses of life.

Dr. Carl Rogers, a clinical psychologist, has studied and written extensively about such relationships. Many of his books are very helpful, especially *On Becoming a Person, Person to Person,* and *Becoming Partners: Marriage and Its Alternatives.*

chapter thirteen

SELF-HYPNOSIS

Hypnosis is a very controversial area. Over the years the popularity of hypnosis in psychological treatment has waxed and waned. In the past hypnosis has, from time to time, received wide attention and endorsement as a legitimate and useful therapeutic tool only to fall into disrepute and disuse with the next generation of psychotherapists. There is currently considerable interest in hypnosis as a tool of treatment. Research is now going on in many important research centers that will enable us to understand the phenomenon better and use it effectively in therapy.

There are two main reasons why hypnosis has waxed and waned over the years. One is that it has often been offered as a panacea for all kinds of problems. When it becomes apparent, after some scrutiny, that it is not a cure-all, many people seem to lose interest. The second reason is that we have never really established just what hypnosis is. Lacking a fully adequate understanding of its nature, many psychologists are reluctant to use it.

Some assert that hypnosis is an altered state of consciousness in which the person goes into a form of trance. This is often thought to give the entranced person some special power to draw on the subconscious, or to alter brain chemistry and functioning. At the other extreme are people who say there is no such thing as hypnosis. They say the subject is just role playing and responding to the suggestions of the hypnotist. These people have conducted research in the area and have been able to demonstrate that they can get their research subjects to do most, if not all, of the things hypnotized subjects do, but without ever hypnotizing the research subjects. Their subjects simply try very hard and are as cooperative as possible.

Before we present an overview of what hypnosis is, it is important to be clear about what it is not. There is hardly an area of psychology that is riddled with as many misconceptions as hypnosis.

First, hypnosis is not a form of sleep. Extensive studies of body reactions of the waking, hypnotic, and sleep states have demonstrated that hypnosis is not sleep, even though hypnotists often used the phrase "You are going to sleep—deep sleep" as part of the hypnotic-induction procedure. Hypnosis is closer to a waking state than to sleep, but it is not identical with being awake either.

Second, the experience of hypnosis is generally not a weird, mysterious, other-worldly experience. Many stage hypnotists who perform primarily for entertainment play up this notion and encourage subjects to feel that way. However, this is not an intrinsic part of the process, and it seldom enters in when hypnosis is used in psychotherapy. It is a very normal, interesting, but unspectacular experience for most people. In fact, many times when I use it with patients, they require reassurance afterwards that they were really hypnotized before they will believe it. It did not have the supernatural quality that they had always thought it would. However, by conducting certain tests of their reactions during the process, it is possible to verify that they were indeed hypnotized.

Third, a person who is hypnotized is not under the power of the hypnotist. He does not surrender his will or lose control of his own behavior. He does become more susceptible to suggestion but basically only to the extent that he wishes to. If the hypnotist suggests that the subject do something to which he has no strong objections, he probably will do it. However, if he suggests something to the subject that the subject really doesn't want to do, he simply won't do it. People are sometimes concerned that a hypnotist will take advantage of a subject and get him to do something antisocial or criminal. This is not possible if the person really doesn't want to do it. However, it is possible to get people to do such things *with or without hypnosis* if they want to or can be persuaded to. Hypnotism has not been found to increase persuasibility toward this kind of behavior very much, if at all. Of course, a responsible hypnotist would not even suggest such a thing in any case. Thus, reports of hypnotism being used to involve people in crime or sexual activity are greatly exaggerated. Hypnotism isn't that powerful. As a precaution, however, against even the possibility, it is wise to deal only with a fully trained and responsible hypnotist such as a clinical psychologist, psychiatrist, or some other professional person.

Many people who think hypnotism has very special power are disappointed when they ask me to hypnotize them and tell them that they won't smoke anymore, drink anymore, or eat so much. It simply doesn't work that way.

Another frequent misconception is that a person does not remember anything about what went on during hypnosis after he wakes up. Actually when the session is over, the hypnotized person generally remembers everything that went on during the session. The only time he doesn't is when he is given specific instructions by the hypnotist to not remember. This is referred to as posthypnotic amnesia. It only occurs when instructions to that effect are given or when the person firmly believes that that will be the effect. Even when the hypnotist gives instructions for posthypnotic amnesia, they don't always work. If the person wants to remember, he generally does. Posthypnotic amnesia is usually not called for in hypnotherapy, but can be very useful on occasion. Often if I am working with a patient on an area that is very upsetting, I will induce posthypnotic amnesia for a period of time during the treatment until we get some of the problems resolved and they are not so painful to think about. This makes the person more comfortable between sessions. In all other cases, they remember everything, and this is best because it facilitates the treatment.

Some people worry that if they become hypnotized they may not be able to wake up. Actually, this never happens. Some people who are hypnotized resist waking up at the end, often because they have found relief and escape in the hypnotic state and don't want to return to real life with its problems. However, this is quite rare.

When it happens, the hypnotist can continue to work on bringing the patient out of it for a time. If that doesn't work, it is best to put him in a comfortable place and wait. Generally he will fall asleep and later wake up alert. Or, he may rest in the hypnotic state for awhile and then voluntarily come out of it. Nobody has gone into a hypnotic state and never come out.

People often say they have tried but can't be hypnotized. Even the scientific literature talks about a certain percentage of people who cannot be hypnotized. However, it depends a lot on how one defines hypnosis. There are levels of hypnosis. Probably everyone, with the possible exception of some severely retarded or greatly emotionally disturbed individuals, can achieve some degree of hypnosis, even if it is very slight.

All right. How can we define hypnosis? First, we have to keep in mind that there is no adequate and perfectly clear definition. We simply don't understand the process well enough to define or explain it fully. However, as a working definition for our purposes, it is useful to think of it as a heightened state of concentration accompanied by an increased ability to act on ideas and suggestions.

It is possible to think of a distraction-concentration continuum. At the extreme distraction end of the continuum people are very inefficient at performing even the simplest tasks. For example, if we had to walk across a stage, pour a glass of water, and give our name and address in front of an audience of 10,000 people, we probably would have great difficulty doing these very simple tasks because of the distraction and anxiety from the audience observing us. We might well stumble across the stage (having forgotten how to walk), pour water on our wrist, throw the glass over our shoulder, and draw a blank on our name and address. At the other end of the continuum, when we are in deep concentration, we become very efficient and can accomplish tasks that are extremely challenging. Our complete concentration and the fact that we are engrossed in the task make it easy for us. Some people are able to get into this state of concentration easily. When they read a book or think about a problem, they shut out all extraneous stimuli from the environment. If you walk into the room and say something to them, they may not even hear you until you go over and shake them. These people are fast readers, good students, and good problem solvers. Other people, of course, are more easily distracted and less efficient in such tasks.

Examples of concentration are plentiful in athletes also. For example, we often talk about a good baseball player being "off at the crack of the bat." When I played baseball, I was able to do that and found that I could reach fly balls that nobody expected me to. I did it by concentrating on the ball while it was still in the pitcher's glove. I then followed it with deep concentration through the wind-up and during its path to the plate. When the ball was hit, I was off at once. In actuality, I was in a type of hypnotic state. Basketball players who stare at the basket, bounce the ball a couple of times, and take a few deep breaths are getting into a similar state before they shoot a foul shot. When they get into that state, crowd noise and attempted distractions do not bother them. They are able to go ahead and make the shot. Pass receivers in football have to have the same ability. If they try to run with the ball before they catch it, they usually drop it. Their concentration has been lost. We also often say, when they drop a pass, that they heard the footsteps behind them—another example of disrupted concentration.

If we view hypnosis as a redistribution of attention, possibly resulting in deeper concentration on selected stimuli, it is easy to see why we can act more readily on suggestions and carry out ideas more efficiently under hypnosis. Viewing hypnosis in this way is a very useful working hypothesis, whether it ultimately proves to be the final answer to the riddle of hypnosis or not. Hypnosis then becomes a way of inducing deeper concentration in ourselves at will, so that we can efficiently carry out tasks we want to.

There are thousands of ways to induce hypnosis. It is relatively easy for a skilled hypnotist to induce the state in a cooperative subject; it is also relatively easy for a person to induce hypnosis in himself.

One simple way to do this is to hold your hand, at arm's length, in front of your face at eye level. Then, stare at a point on the hand. It can be any point such as a knuckle, ring, or freckle. The important thing is focusing vision on a spot. Then, move the hand slowly toward your forehead and bring the point being focused on up to the forehead right between your eyes. When your hand touches your forehead, close your eyes, and go through the relaxation procedure outlined in chapter two. At this point you will be completely relaxed and your eyes will be closed. Now, begin to count and with each count let your body relax a little more and go a little deeper into the state of hypnosis. Beginners may want to count to 45 or 50. With a little practice you will be able to achieve satisfactory results by counting to only 10 or 15. At the end of this procedure you will be in a light state of hypnosis. An alternate procedure is to roll the eyes back into the head as far as you can for a few seconds (rather than focusing on the hand and moving it to the forehead). Follow this with the same relaxation and counting procedure as above.

Once you achieve a light state of hypnosis, you can use it to relieve anxiety. One way is simply to tell yourself that you are going to calm down and get things under control. You will often find that this works wonders. When you wake up you will feel much better, less tense, and more relaxed.

You can also think through problems in this state and figure out ways to handle them. The relaxation and freedom from distraction will facilitate good problem solving.

In this state you can also tell yourself things that you know are true and would like to accept emotionally but have not been able to convince yourself of while awake. Hypnosis will make you more able to respond to such ideas or suggestions. For example, you might say to yourself, "I'm going to interview for that job next week. There is no need to be overly anxious about it. It is normal to be a little tense in such a situation and I'll be that. But, I'll be amazingly more relaxed than before. After all, the interview isn't that important. If I get the job, fine. If not, there is no sense in being anxious about it. Being calm will actually enhance my chances and make me more likely to handle the interview well and get the job. I'll be very calm. If I don't get it, maybe next time." Under hypnosis you can talk to yourself and tell yourself things of this sort. They will have a greater impact and be more believable. It's amazingly simple, but it works.

Some people also like to think about pleasant or calm situations and experiences under hypnosis. This is very similar to the meditation exercises discussed in chapter three. There is great similarity between hypnosis and meditation. In fact, many of the feats of the yogis and other mystics are probably attributable to a type of hypnotic process.

After you have used hypnosis to help reduce your anxiety, it is simple to wake up. You simply say, "I am now going to wake up. I will feel refreshed, relaxed, and wide awake. My mind will be clear and I will feel good all over." Then, open your eyes. You will feel as if you have just awakened from a nap or stopped working on something that completely engrossed your interest. It is a pleasant and exhilarating experience.

A word or two of caution is called for here. If hypnosis seems frightening to you or you are unsure of it, don't do it. It should be a pleasant, helpful experience. If it frightens you before you try it or if it seems to have that effect when you try it, stop. Under such circumstances, it is best to consult a professionally trained hypnotist before going on. He may work with you and help you get over your fear, or he may tell you that hypnosis is not for you at this time. If you have tried self-hypnosis and it didn't seem to work very well for you, it is also best to consult a professionally trained person. To find a qualified professional hypnotist, call the chairman of the psychology department at a nearby college or the head of the psychiatry department of a nearby medical school.

chapter fourteen

PROFESSIONAL HELP

After reading this book and trying some of the techniques that seem to fit your situation best, you may find that you are still experiencing more anxiety than you would like to. You would like to be more calm about things and relaxed enough to enjoy life rather than having it be such a struggle. Sometimes the anxiety may be related to a specific situation which will change after a short period of time. If that is the case, it may be best just to wait it out, much as you would a cold or some similar minor ailment. Everyone has short periods of stress and anxiety from time to time that have to be endured just as other unpleasant things in life. However, if your anxiety is persistent, it may be best for you to seek help from a professional counselor or psychotherapist. Your problems may be such that they need more than can be offered in a book like this. Or, you may simply need a little help from someone with more experience in implementing the techniques outlined in this book. In any event, if you decide to seek professional help, there are some points worth considering. The first place people go with this type of problem is to their family physician or to their minister. They can be very helpful, especially if the anxiety is relatively minor and not related to more serious problems.

The physician has had little or no training in psychological counseling, but he can often offer reassurance and advice based on the wisdom growing out of his involvement with many people's lives. He can also prescribe medications that will reduce the discomfort you may be experiencing. These medications will be discussed in more detail later in this chapter.

Some ministers are trained in counseling and can be very helpful, others do not have training or skills in these areas. The important thing to keep in mind is that the family physician and the minister are prepared to help with only minor, short-term anxiety problems. Their major training and skills lie in other areas. For people with more serious anxiety problems, the best source of help is generally a clinical psychologist or a psychiatrist. Numerous surveys have shown that most people are uncertain about what difference there is between these two.

A clinical psychologist is generally a person who has earned a doctoral degree in psychology, with specialization in the areas of psychopathology, diagnostic evaluation, treatment of people with emotional disturbances, and related areas. This requires approximately twenty years of academic training as well as thousands of hours of practical training and experience. The clinical psychologist generally completes twelve years of elementary and secondary school, four years of undergraduate training in psychology and four or more years of graduate training in psychology. During the graduate training, in addition to his courses, he works in treatment settings such as hospitals and clinics under supervision of more experienced psychologists. He then completes a year of internship and frequently undergoes an additional year or more of supervision of his work after the doctoral degree is awarded. At this point, he can be licensed to offer services on an independent basis to the public. He is trained and experienced in the basic sciences pertaining to diagnosis and treatment of emotional disturbances.

The psychiatrist is a physician who has decided to specialize in the treatment of people suffering from emotional disturbances. He, therefore, completes twelve years of elementary and secondary school, followed by three or four years of undergraduate college, three or four years of medical school, a year of internship, and generally a two- or three-year psychiatric residency. As a resident he serves on the staff of a hospital or clinic and receives additional training and supervision in the treatment of emotional disturbance.

In terms of the rigor and extensiveness of their training, clinical psychologists and psychiatrists have essentially equivalent backgrounds. Both training programs are highly competitive, require a high degree of ability and diligence to complete, and take about the same number of years. The main difference is that one produces a psychologist who has decided to specialize in treatment of emotionally disturbed individuals rather than one of the other areas of psychology, while the other produces a physician who has decided to specialize in treatment of the emotionally disturbed rather than in one of the other areas of medicine. In most of their routine clinical practice psychologists and psychiatrists function very similarly. However, since their backgrounds are different, they do bring different skills to a situation. The physician is highly trained in the physical functioning of the body and is licensed to prescribe drugs. The psychologist is more highly trained in psychological functioning, personality theory, psychological diagnostic testing, and research. In many settings psychologists and psychiatrists work together in teams to capitalize on the unique skills of each. In independent private practice, they generally develop cooperative relationships to accomplish the same thing. For example, if a psychiatrist has a difficult diagnostic decision to make, he will frequently refer the patient to a psychologist for an extensive personality evaluation using psychological tests before the diagnosis is made. Likewise, if a patient of a psychologist has a physical problem or needs medication, he will have a physician see the patient and attend to this aspect. Both clinical psychologists and psychiatrists offer excellent help for the emotionally disturbed.

Another type of practitioner that people often wonder about is the psychoanalyst. A psychoanalyst is a professionally trained person (usually a clinical psychologist or psychiatrist) who has had additional training and experience in the application of Freudian theory to the treatment of emotional disturbance. This usually involves two or three additional years of training and a personal psychoanalysis for the person before he becomes a psychoanalyst for other people. Psychoanalysis generally requires several meetings a week for several years. Each session costs from $25 to $200, depending on the going rate in the area, the eminence of the therapist, and your ability to pay. Due to the time and expense involved in psychoanalysis, it is generally not indicated except for rather serious problems. In recent years the efficacy and efficiency of psychoanalytic treatment has come under serious question. Many psychologists and psychiatrists currently feel that the beneficial results are not sufficient to justify the time and expense required.

Another approach that is gaining in popularity is called behavior therapy. It has been developed primarily in the last fifteen or twenty years and draws heavily on research from psychological laboratories throughout the world. Numerous investigations have demonstrated that these newer treatments work effectively and in a relatively short period of time in bringing relief from many types of emotional disturbance. Many of the ideas presented in this book are based on behavior therapy techniques.

Once you have decided to see a professional psychotherapist, the problem becomes one of choosing the person you want to see. They are, of course, listed in the yellow pages of the phone book, and friends can often recommend someone they know. However, you may also want to check with the local psychological or medical societies for names. There are also state psychological and state medical associations. A little inquiry and some help from the telephone information operator will help you locate their office. Another good way to look for a psychologist is to write or call the chairman of the psychology department of a nearby college or university or the department of psychiatry at a nearby medical school if you wish to see a psychiatrist. Tell them the general nature of your problem and the type of psychotherapist you would like to see. They are generally quite willing to help.

As noted earlier in this chapter, certain types of medication are used to reduce anxiety. Actually, there are two major types of medication generally prescribed by physicians in such cases. These are sedatives and tranquilizers. Sedatives have their effect by inhibiting and depressing the activity of the central nervous system (brain and spinal cord). They generally make a person feel calm. Some of the better known brand names of these drugs are Eskabarb,

Miltown, Equanil, Librium, Valium, and Serax. While these are technically sedatives as defined by their sedating effect on the central nervous system, they are often loosely referred to as tranquilizers or minor tranquilizers. Most of the real tranquilizers or major tranquilizers are chemically phenothiazine derivatives. Commonly known brand names of these are Thorazine, Mellaril, Stelazine, Trilafon, and Prolixin. How these drugs have their effect is not completely understood, but they seem to affect centers of the brain that are involved in expressing emotional behavior. When the emotion-mediating centers of the brain are better controlled, the person feels more tranquil and less confused.

Usually sedatives, or minor tranquilizers, are used in cases of simple tension and anxiety. Major tranquilizers are used when the patient's agitation is accompanied by symptoms of thought disturbance, confusion, hostile or aggressive behavior, and other more serious forms of emotional disturbance. However, these are very general guidelines, and there may be very good reasons for prescribing them in a variety of circumstances. It is best to trust your physician's judgment as to what is best for you at the time.

Most people do not know that alcohol as found in the traditional alcoholic beverages of beer, wine, and whiskey is chemically a sedative drug. It has essentially the same effect as the drugs mentioned above, which are prescribed by a physician. As we are well aware, in our culture, alcohol is a greatly abused and overused drug. The reason for this is that alcohol is a fast-acting, short-term sedative. Thus, the sedative effects of the drug occur very shortly after ingestion. But they also wear off before long. Therefore, to maintain the effect, we must drink more. The body habituates to such drugs. So, before very long, larger and more frequent doses are required to get the same effect. At this rate the person is apt to find himself *addicted* to alcohol. It's a familiar pattern.

Thus, the important thing to keep in mind is that alcohol is a drug, specifically a sedative, and one that we can become addicted to. Therefore, it is best not to use it as a self-medication. When we have anxieties and tensions, we should learn to handle them by using the techniques presented earlier in this book. If we need medication, we should see a physician. He can prescribe a safer medication that will work better. By using it under his care, we can be assured that there is much less likelihood of our abusing the drug and becoming addicted. We should not take alcoholic beverages to relieve anxiety. That is too dangerous. If taken at all, alcoholic beverages are best in moderate amounts with meals or on social occasions for our added pleasure rather than as desperate attempts to escape from pain and anxiety.

Another very important point is that drugs frequently interact with each other when taken together. Many times two drugs that are quite safe and helpful if taken separately can become extremely potent and dangerous if taken together. Alcohol is very much this way with some of the sedatives and tranquilizers mentioned above. If one takes a small dose of some of these medications and then drinks a few ounces of alcohol, the combined effect can cause the person to be dangerously slow in reactions, making driving, working, or other activities very hazardous. He may also lose consciousness and in some cases even die as a result. Be very careful about taking medications with each other or with alcohol. Ask your physician before you do.

One other form of self-medication should be mentioned. There are various patented medicines on the market that are available in drugstores without a prescription. They are sold to relieve tension and to aid in going to sleep. Most of these contain small doses of antihistamines, which are known to produce a sedative effect. Many of them also contain other mild sedative agents, small amounts of pain-relieving medications, and sometimes vitamins. If you are experiencing very mild and temporary tension and anxiety, these are certainly worth a try. They often help greatly and make stronger measures unnecessary. Your druggist can help you select one. They are safe and very economical. Be sure to use them as directed on the package.

The medications discussed above are primarily palliative rather than curative. That is, they will make you feel a little better temporarily, but they do not cure or clear up the problem. If the anxiety is brief and infrequent, they can be very helpful. However, if it persists or comes back too often, chances are you need psychotherapeutic treatment by a clinical psychologist or psychiatrist. The sooner you find one and begin to work on your problems, the sooner you will feel better.

One final point should be mentioned before we end this book. That is that many people who work very hard alone or with professional help at reducing anxiety often report that when the anxiety begins to go down, depression begins to increase. This occurs only in a small number of cases, and it should not be a matter of great concern. Usually what has happened is that the person has been so accustomed to living under great tension or pressure, that a normal anxiety-free state seems flat and drab. Then they get depressed. Generally, if one is patient, the depression will leave. It helps to involve yourself in things you enjoy and begin to make life more interesting and exciting. The points made in chapter eleven can be helpful. If the depression is unusually severe or persistent, you should contact a professional psychotherapist.

Be cool.

INDEX

INDEX

A

Activating Events (A), 27, 28
Aerobics, 77
Aggression, 3
   vs. assertion, 61
Alcohol, 106–107
Alternatives, evaluation of, 70–71
Anxiety:
   ABC's of, 27
   anticipatory, 42–43
   definition, 1–3
   • free floating, 4
   irrational, 31, 36, 44
   motivation from, 4
   spiral, 19, 20
   unconscious, 4
*Anxiety and Tension Control: A
   Physiologic Approach* (Jacobson), 25
Assertion training, 60

B

Baths:
   alternating hot and cold, 79
   hot, 79
   sauna, rules, 79–80
   steam, rules, 79–80
*Becoming Partners: Marriage and
   Its Alternatives* (Rogers), 94
Behavior rehearsal, 15, 16, 65
Behavior therapy, 105
Belief System (B), faulty, irra-
   tional, 27, 28, 29, 31
Biofeedback, 18
Brainstorming, 68–70

C

Carnegie, Dale, 65
Catastrophizing, 28, 32

Parkinson's Law, 86
Pasteur, Louis, 29
Peale, Norman Vincent, 60, 65
Perfection, 31, 35–36
Perls, Fritz, 90
Person to Person (Rogers), 94
Phobia, 3
Physician, 76, 77, 78, 79, 102, 103,
    104, 107
Planning, 14, 46, 49, 51
Play, 83–84, 86
Positive thinking, 65
Power of Positive Thinking, The
    (Peale), 65
Process, 56
Procrastination, 34, 59
Psychiatrist:
    locating one, 17, 105
    training, 103–104
Psychoanalyst, 104
Psychocybernetics (Maltz), 65
Psychologist:
    locating one, 17, 105
    training, 103–104
Punishment, 31, 64

R

Rational-Emotive Therapy, 27
Recreation, 83
Reinforcement, 55–56, 64, 72, 86,
    91
Relaxation procedures, 10, 12, 14,
    20, 21
    (see also Differential relaxation)
Rogers, Carl, 94

S

Sedatives, 105, 107
Self-confidence, 34, 72
Suffering, 40-41
Systematic desensitizations:
    in imagination, 11, 16
    for unique events, 16
    in vivo, 13, 16

T

Tension, 3
Thought stopping, 57
Three Pillars of Zen, The
    (Kapleau), 25
Time, 41–42
To a Dancing God (Keen), 82
Tranquilizers, 105–106, 107
Trust, 92

U

Unconditional positive regard, 90
Unitas, Johnny, 29

V

Values:
    attitudinal, 40–42
    creative, 39–40
    experiential, 40
Vitamins, 76